GARFIELD COUNTY LIBRARIES
Parachute Branch Library
244 Grand Valley Way
Parachute, CO 81635
(970) 285-9870 • Fax (970) 285-7477
www.gcpld.org

Brought to you by
the passage of 2018
ballot measure 6A.

Thank you voters!

GARFIELD COUNTY
LIBRARIES

INVEST FOR GOOD

INVEST FOR GOOD

A Healthier World and a Wealthier You

MARK MOBIUS, CARLOS VON HARDENBERG & GREG KONIECZNY

BLOOMSBURY BUSINESS
LONDON • NEW YORK • OXFORD • NEW DELHI • SYDNEY

BLOOMSBURY BUSINESS
Bloomsbury Publishing Plc
50 Bedford Square, London, WC1B 3DP, UK
1385 Broadway, New York, NY 10018, USA

BLOOMSBURY, BLOOMSBURY BUSINESS and the Diana logo are
trademarks of Bloomsbury Publishing Plc

First published in Great Britain 2019

Cover design: Eleanor Rose
Cover image © Getty Images

A catalogue record for this book is available from the British Library.

A catalog record for this book is available from the Library of Congress.

ISBN: HB: 978-1-4729-6265-2
       ePDF: 978-1-4729-6267-6
       eBook: 978-1-4729-6266-9

Typeset by RefineCatch Limited, Bungay, Suffolk
Printed and bound in Great Britain

To find out more about our authors and books visit www.bloomsbury.com
and sign up for our newsletters.

MIX
Paper from
responsible sources
FSC® C013604

CONTENTS

PREFACE

The idea of this book began germinating in the autumn of 2017, when the authors snatched a few hours from their globetrotting lives as investors in emerging markets, to step back from their jobs and discuss wider issues.

They agreed that two changes, in particular, were destabilising the status quo and generating both risks and opportunities for the professional investor. The first was the rapid growth in recent years of 'passive' funds, so called because they substitute low-cost index-tracking investment for active investor engagement with portfolio companies. The second profound change, which is, in some ways, a mirror image of the first, is the equally rapid growth in recent years of so-called 'ESG' (environment, social, governance) investing. While the growth of passive investing is tantamount to a wholesale withdrawal of investors from engagement with portfolio companies, the growth of ESG investing is tantamount to demands by investors that portfolio companies should act in environmentally and socially responsible ways, while adhering to high standards of corporate governance.

Having identified the growth of passive and ESG investment as leitmotifs of the development of fund management in the early twenty-first century, the authors turned their attention to the implications for investment in emerging markets. They knew that the encroachment of ever larger passive funds was less pronounced in emerging markets for two reasons: because active investing in emerging markets was still producing very strong returns, and because passive investing was fundamentally unsuited to these less liquid and less efficient markets. They knew, too, that ESG investing faced more challenges in the emerging than in the mature markets, because of the relative lack of information and regulation and, consequently, a relative lack of companies in emerging markets that could pass or could be seen to pass the ESG tests.

In the light of these sea changes in investing, in general, and investing in emerging markets, in particular, the authors decided on two courses of action: set up a new company dedicated to active investing in emerging and frontier markets, with the aim to improve companies by focussing particularly on the 'G' component, i.e. the way companies deal with corporate governance; and to write a book, this book, explaining why their approach is likely to succeed in emerging and 'frontier' markets and how they plan to implement their strategy.

The authors believe they are well qualified for both endeavours. Dr Mark Mobius, co-founder of Mobius Capital Partners (MCP), has spent over 40 years seeking out and actively managing investments in emerging and frontier markets. Before launching MCP in March 2018, Mark worked for the Franklin Templeton Investments fund management company, latterly as executive chairman of Templeton Emerging Markets Group. During his tenure, the group expanded assets under management from US$100 million to over US$40 billion, and launched a number of emerging market and frontier funds, including private equity funds as well as open- and closed-end mutual funds.

Mark has played an important role in the development of international policy on emerging markets. In 1999, he was asked to serve on the World Bank's Global Corporate Governance Forum as a member of the Private Sector Advisory Group and was co-chairman of its Investor Responsibility Task Force. He is also a member of the Economic Advisory Board of the International Finance Corporation. He has also been on the supervisory board of OMV Petrom in Romania since 2010, and is a former non-executive director of Lukoil, the Russian oil company.

As undisputed doyen of emerging markets investment, Mark has been honoured with many industry awards and plaudits, including the Lifetime Achievement Award in Asset Management by Global Investor Magazine (2017); being ranked by *Bloomberg Markets Magazine* as one of the 50 Most Influential People (2011); an Africa Investor Index Series Award (2010); and being ranked by Asiamoney among the Top 100 Most Powerful and Influential People (2006). In 2007, he was featured in the comic book *Mark Mobius: An Illustrated Biography*.

Carlos von Hardenberg, one of Mobius Capital Partners' three founding partners, has 19 years of experience in financial markets, of which 17 were spent with Franklin Templeton Investments, where he started as a research analyst based in Singapore and focused on South East Asia. He lived and worked in Poland before settling in Istanbul, Turkey, for 10 years. Carlos has spent a great deal of his time travelling in Asia, Latin America, Africa and Eastern Europe, visiting companies and identifying investment targets.

He managed country, regional and global emerging and frontier market portfolios. Carlos was appointed lead manager of London Stock Exchange-listed Templeton Emerging Market Trust in 2015, where he delivered significant out-performance. He established and managed one of the largest global frontier market funds of recent years. Before joining Franklin Templeton, Carlos worked as a corporate finance analyst for Bear Stearns International in London and New York.

Greg Konieczny, the other founding partner of Mobius Capital Partners, has over 25 years of experience in financial markets, of which 22 years were spent at Franklin Templeton Investments, where he was recruited by Mark to conduct research into and manage Templeton Emerging Markets Group investments in Eastern Europe.

In 2010, Greg became fund manager of Fondul Proprietatea, the largest Romanian closed-end investment fund, and one of the largest London-listed funds, with US$ 2.7 billion in net assets. The fund included large minority interests in private and state-controlled Romanian blue-chip companies. During his seven-year engagement, he and his team in Bucharest helped to transform corporate governance standards in many of the portfolio companies, which contributed to significant improvements in their financial results and to increases in market valuations.

In his role as Director of Specialty Strategies for the whole of Templeton Emerging Markets Group, Greg was responsible for specialised country and regional strategies for Emerging Markets. He and his team engaged with large portfolio companies in various sectors and regions to improve their governance. Before joining Franklin Templeton, Greg worked for three years at Bank Gdanski, one of the largest financial institutions in Poland at the time.

It goes without saying that, with eight decades of experience in emerging markets investing between them, the authors write with some authority on the issues, ideas and concepts addressed in this book. However, given that an implication of the environmental element of ESG investing is that most books would be better left as trees, why is this book – and, for that matter, a brand new fund management company, Mobius Capital Partners – necessary, and why now?

There are two answers to these questions.

The first is that the authors are worried about the seemingly unstoppable advance of passive investing. They acknowledge that its low management fees are attractive to investors, but they regard it as a threat to economic development. When investors take no interest in the companies they invest in and blindly track some share index instead, they can exert no influence on the allocation of capital between companies, sectors or countries. And it is the allocations of capital we make today that determines the kind of world we will live in tomorrow.

At a time when passive exchange-traded funds seem to be sweeping all before them, the authors want to stand up for and proclaim the virtues of active investment and its allocative power.

The second answer to 'Why this book, why now?' is that ESG as a template for investor choice, which the authors are committed to and approve of, is still in its infancy. Despite all the hype, ESG investing remains a largely European phenomenon, and its dominant instrument remains 'negative screening': excluding companies that do not pass ESG tests from portfolios. The authors believe that the full beneficial potential of ESG investing will not be realised until it is combined with the active investment approach and its writ is extended to the emerging markets, where its impact on management and governance can do the most good.

ACKNOWLEDGEMENTS

We would like to thank Tom Lloyd for his excellent support in writing this book. It is certainly not easy to work with three authors who are travelling all over the world and are seldom in one place at one time but Tom, in his calm and professional manner, has made the impossible possible.

We would also like to thank Anna von Hahn for her invaluable help in coordinating the project and ensuring we stayed focussed!

Finally, a great thank you to the excellent team at Bloomsbury Business for guiding us so professionally through the publication process. Our book could not have been in better hands.

ABBREVIATIONS

CalPERS	California Public Employees' Retirement System
CCC	Clean Clothes Campaign
CEDAW	Convention on the Elimination of All Forms of Discrimination Against Women
CEO	chief executive officer
CFO	chief financial officer
CFP	corporate financial performance
CPI	Corruption Perceptions Index (Transparency International)
CRP	country risk premium
DfID	Department for International Development (UK)
ERISA	Employee Retirement Income Security Act (USA)
ESG	environment, social, governance
ETF	exchange-traded fund
Eurosif	European Sustainable Investment Forum
FT	France Télécom
GDP	gross domestic product
Generation Z	born in mid-1990s and afterwards
GFI	Global Financial Integrity

GHGs	greenhouse gases
GRI	Global Reporting Initiative
GSIA	Global Sustainable Investment Alliance
GSM	general shareholder meeting
IFC	International Finance Corporation (World Bank Group)
IIRC	International Integrated Reporting Council
ILO	International Labour Organization
ISS	Institutional Shareholder Services
KPI	key performance indicator
Millennials	born in the 1980s and early 1990s
MSCI	Morgan Stanley Capital International
MSCI ACWI	MSCI All Country World Index
NASDAQ	National Association of Securities Dealers Automated Quotations
OECD	Organisation for Economic Co-operation and Development
PwC	PricewaterhouseCoopers
RVMs	Reverse-vending machines
SASB	Sustainability Accounting Standards Board
SEC	Securities and Exchange Commission (USA and Poland)
SRI	socially responsible investing

TPSA	Telekomunikacja Polska SA
UN PRI	United Nations Principles for Responsible Investment
UN SDGs	United Nations Sustainable Development Goals
UNFCCC	United Nations Framework Convention on Climate Change
URS	universal recycling symbol

Introduction

'Is there money in it?' asked a delegate to a conference early in 2018 when Mark told her about Mobius Capital Partners' mission to bring the gospel of active 'ESG' investing to emerging markets.

Mark's questioner was not displaying her ignorance about what 'ESG' stood for. She knew very well that 'ESG investing' is taking 'environmental, social and governance' factors into account when making investment decisions. Nor could she have been in any doubt about the meaning of the term 'active', in this context. She would have known that, when applied to investing, 'active' means a policy of engagement with portfolio companies as opposed to 'passive' index-tracking.

Her underlying question was: 'Can ESG investing in general, and active ESG investing in particular, achieve a reasonable return in emerging markets?'

As we shall see, the evidence suggests the answer to the first part of her question is, 'Yes'; ESG investing is actually slightly more profitable than non-ESG investing. The evidence also suggests that active investing is more profitable than passive investing. The third part of the question (can active ESG investing make good financial returns in the so-called emerging markets?), can also be answered provisionally in the affirmative, although there is rather less corroborating evidence for this conclusion.

It is hard to exaggerate the impact those three little letters 'ESG' are having on the global investment community as we approach the third decade of the twenty-first century. The abbreviation is on everyone's lips, and declarations of allegiance by funds and companies to the philosophy of business it expresses are almost daily occurrences.

Pleas for a more responsible approach to investment that were once unheard voices in the wilderness from single-issue pressure groups, with no apparent understanding of fund managers' fiduciary duties to their beneficiaries, have become mainstream. By bundling together thin threads dating back centuries in some cases, ESG has set the scene for the emergence of a new contract between business and society being promoted by a formidable cast of actors.

In order of appearance, the 'dramatis personae' have included: eighteenth-century Puritans disgusted by the evils of alcohol and tobacco and vehemently opposed to the Atlantic slave trade; 'baby-boomer' ecologists and environmentalists in the 1960s, with their communes and dreams of self-sufficiency; the anti-apartheid campaigners of the 1980s; and the United Nations (UN) with the publication of *Our Common Future* (also known as the *Brundtland Report*) by the World Commission on Environment and Development in 1987.

Today, this ensemble also includes: companies with Corporate Social Responsibility (CSR) programmes and commitments to lowering their carbon footprints; governments with ever tighter environmental and social laws and regulations; self-regulatory bodies that issue a constant stream of new, ESG-related disclosure and reporting requirements; charities and foundations that focus on environmental degradation or social deprivation; a new breed of so-called 'impact' investors who combine elements of charitable and commercial investment; ESG index compilers, analysts and consultants trying to give numerical substance to ESG performance; passive ESG index-tracker funds; and 'active' investors who prod their portfolio companies towards ESG compliance.

But the star of the ESG show, in which all the other actors play their parts, is none of these. It is not a person or an organisation. It is a generation: the 'millennial' generation, born in the 1980s and 1990s. It is their general outlook and world view, their impending grasp of the reins of power, their fastidious consumption (exemplified by their appetite for products carrying the Fairtrade logo and packaging carrying the universal recycling symbol, URS), their mastery of modern social media and their insatiable curiosity, that have endowed ESG with its economic and political power.

Another reason why ESG has moved centre stage in investing now is that the millennials are better informed than their parents and are lifting the veil of investor ignorance.

Investors have been disadvantaged by ignorance ever since the serpent persuaded Adam to dabble in the fresh fruit market. A lack of knowledge about the businesses and ventures they have invested in made them easy prey for swindlers, embezzlers, unscrupulous share promoters and incompetent or corrupt managers. The collapse of the South Sea Company in 1720 led to the destitution of so many of its investors that the British government felt obliged to pass the 'Bubble' Act, limiting the liability of investors to the sums they had invested.

The problem of ignorance and the risks that accompany it have eased over the centuries as information has become more accessible and corporate reporting requirements have become tighter. But huge sums of money are still lost each year by investors who do not know enough about the companies and ventures in which they invest.

The explosion of information ignited by the Internet, and its universal availability through computers and smartphones, has the potential to illuminate much that was previously hidden and to reduce investor ignorance and the risks associated with it.

But although old questions can be answered more easily in this richer information environment, there are new questions, many of them to do with ESG, that are harder to answer. The millennials want to be sure the companies they buy from, work for and invest in are good, kind and responsible, and have 'sustainable' business models. For millennial investors, it is no longer enough for their portfolio companies to make money for them.

The problems of ESG measurement are particularly acute in the emerging markets, where disclosure requirements are less strict and less diligently policed. It has been estimated, for instance, that fewer than 50 per cent of all Asian companies disclose carbon emissions, against 90 per cent of European companies. With some honourable exceptions, emerging market countries also tend to rank lower in Transparency International's 'Corruption Perceptions Index' (CPI) and their companies are less transparent than companies in mature markets. Because of this relative lack of reliable information about emerging market companies, the passive funds that now dominate the fund-management market tend to steer clear of emerging markets. They declare their allegiance to ESG in principle, but their low-cost business models oblige them to rely, for their ESG credentials, on tracking a new breed of ESG indices that do not cover emerging markets as well as they cover mature markets. This is a pity in our view, because it is in emerging markets where investor pressure on companies to comply with ESG principles can do the most good. In areas of the world where broad-brush screening, specialist ESG indices and desk research alone cannot reach, active investing (going to companies and seeing for yourselves) is the only way to obtain enough information to take properly calculated risks.

Emerging markets are the modern investment frontier. Like the Wild West of America in the nineteenth century, they offer the investor a classic combination of high-risk and high-potential reward. Active investing, our kind of investing, is the only key that can unlock the treasure in the corporate sectors of emerging markets.

There is nothing new about 'active' investing or about active investing in emerging markets. The development we focus on in this book is the application of the ESG principles to active investing in emerging markets. ESG investing, or 'sustainable' investing, as it is also known, is the beacon that guides us as we try to ensure that the deployment of the funds in our care reflects the desires of our investors for stable, well-governed societies and companies and for the ecological integrity of what Buckminster Fuller called 'Spaceship Earth'. This book is a manifesto, not for our company, but for active, ESG investing in the emerging markets generally, in an investment world dominated by passively managed funds. Active investors bring about change. Passive investors simply preserve the status quo.

We begin in Chapter 1 with an account of the origins of Socially Responsible Investing (SRI) and some other precursors of ESG investing, including the UN's six Principles for Responsible Investment (UN PRI), and, for the emerging markets, the UN's 17 Sustainable Development Goals. We describe the state and scale of the ESG art today, before concluding with a quick, conceptual tour around 'E', 'S' and 'G' and a brief discussion of their relative importance and how they interact with each other.

Chapter 2 focuses on the first two dimensions of ESG: E and S (environment and society). It gives accounts of their origins and sets out the key issues and options for investors. We distinguish between negative and positive screening and point to some of the dilemmas investors face when considering actions or policies that inflict damage on one component of ESG while conferring benefit on another.

In Chapter 3, we turn our attention to the third dimension of ESG: G (governance). We look at changing patterns of corruption in emerging markets, tracked by Transparency International, highlight the links between corruption and economic growth, and tell stories of our own encounters, as investors, with corporate corruption. We go on to describe other governance issues such as the lack of gender equality as well as other problems that are caused by excessively close links between business and politics.

Chapter 4 is about reforming governance, at both the national and corporate levels. We look at the relationship between national (macro) and corporate (micro) governance reform with the help of examples in Eastern Europe.

Chapter 5 is about 'active' investing. It describes how, at a time when 'passive' investing seems to be carrying all before it, the hunger of companies and governments everywhere for capital gives active investors considerable power over how companies and governments conduct themselves. We give some prominent examples of successful exercises of this investor power, note the commitments to ESG of some of the world's largest funds and tell the tales of some of our own successes and failures in exercising our power as active investors in emerging markets.

In Chapter 6, we describe the 'continuum' of investors in the emerging markets, ranging from charities and aid programmes to the new breed of 'impact' investors to active investors, like us. We suggest the continuum is a ladder, or hierarchy, up which emerging market companies must climb, if they are to become integrated with the global economy. We discuss the role of multinational companies as emerging market investors, through their local subsidiaries and associates, and recount our experiences as their co-investors. We draw a distinction between 'financial' and 'psychological' returns on investment, and suggest that the balance between the two differs, at different levels of the hierarchy.

Fund performance and the challenges of measurement in the ESG area are addressed in Chapter 7. We refer to recent research that suggests that despite the fact that ESG investors are motivated by 'psychological' as well as financial returns, they have not so far had to pay a penalty in financial return for their insistence on ESG compliance. We assess the roles of the measurers and trackers of ESG investment, including non-governmental organisations (NGOs), compilers and publishers of ESG indices, analysts and consultants, foundations and gatherers of raw data, including various kinds of investor.

The book ends in Chapter 8 with some speculations about the long-term impact of sustainable ESG investing on emerging markets. Could it lead to a more stable, peaceful, prosperous Africa, for instance, or to reduced poverty, higher growth rates and greater productivity? Will it help to improve living standards in emerging markets? Is it reasonable to see active ESG investing in emerging markets as an important contributor to the achievement of the UN's Sustainable Development Goals?

'Sustainable' ESG investment is coming of age. In more mature markets, it is fast becoming such an important part of the corporate environment that no company can continue to ignore ESG prejudices and judgements when drafting plans or strategies. For the first time since the emergence of the joint stock company, the owners of publicly listed companies are learning how to flex their muscles and to spell out clearly and forcefully what 'good' looks like in the corporate species.

This pressure will only increase. A survey by US Trust showed that three-quarters of 'millennials' put a high priority on social goals when they invest; that is in stark contrast to baby boomers, where the proportion was only a third. In the USA, millennials are the largest living generation. They are twice as likely as baby boomers to regard political, environmental and social impact as 'somewhat' or 'extremely' important when making their investment decisions, and they are more than twice as likely as baby boomers (76 vs 36 per cent) to see their investment decisions as a way to express their values (I.1).

It does not seem unreasonable to infer from these results that millennials want to invest their money in places where their ESG values will have the most impact. We believe that those places are the emerging markets.

ESG investing is not a passing fad. It is a permanent addition to the environment within which companies raise capital. With over $20 trillion of professionally managed investment funds worldwide paying at least passive lip-service to ESG principles, it is not a genie that can be pushed back into its bottle. It is based on the solid evidence of investors' eyes and ears. Human inquisitiveness and modern communications technology and habits have lifted those veils of ignorance that once obscured the environmental and social impacts of corporate activity. People can see in documentaries and Internet clips the harm plastic waste is inflicting on our oceans, rivers and public places. Readily available satellite imagery shows the alarming contraction of rainforests and coral reefs as well as the equally alarming expansion of the world's deserts. The Sahara Desert in Africa, for example, is estimated to have grown by over 1.5 million square kilometres in barely a century. The Gobi Desert in China is thought to be growing by over 3,000 square kilometres a year. People smell air pollution or see others on television and social media breathing through face masks.

The proliferation of news channels, blogs and the mass-market social media platforms exposes the sweatshops and human trafficking associated with global supply chains. Corrupt corporations everywhere, in mature as well as emerging markets, are fast running out of places to hide.

ESG investing does not solve these problems, but it is pushing in the right direction. It is a force for good in the world.

1

The idea of the good company

We were travelling by car along a dusty, potholed road on our way to a meeting with the executives of a Nigerian oil refiner. The air conditioning was working overtime in the blistering heat. Progress was slow because an oil tanker we were following was threading its way very carefully round the large potholes. With a hiss and the mechanical knock of air brakes, the tanker stopped suddenly, swaying briefly on its shock absorbers. Our driver hit the brakes and we skidded a few yards to a halt.

We waited.

A few moments later, two young men in their teens emerged from bushes at the side of the road, each carrying a 10 gallon plastic jerrycan. Looking neither right nor left, they walked to the back of the tanker, opened a spigot, filled their once white containers with what looked like crude oil, closed the spigot and disappeared back into the bushes with their booty.

The air brakes hissed off and the tanker resumed its journey.

As our driver released the handbrake on his nearly new VW and followed the now slightly depleted tanker, we looked at each other and exchanged wry smiles. We had both been reminded of another oil company in Eastern Europe we had invested in a few years back that had been similarly plundered, albeit less openly (see p. 61).

It was like being in a time warp, watching a modern equivalent of a stagecoach being robbed by outlaws, in broad daylight, with the apparent connivance of the tanker driver. It had not escaped our notice that the oil tanker was emblazoned with the logo of the company we were calling on, and in which we had been thinking of investing. For us, the visitors from the future, this seemed to be evidence of violations of all three of the ESG principles.

After two more identical stop-and-steal halts, Carlos began to fear this could be a wasted visit. He had identified the company as a potential investment, but was now having second thoughts. If the company tolerated such blatant theft, aided and abetted by the oil tanker's driver, there had to be concerns about the quality of its management and governance. He said as much to me.

'Should we call and cancel the meeting?' he asked.

'No,' I said. 'We're nearly there now. Let's hear what they have to say...'

Before hearing what our hosts had to say, let us travel back in time and retrace the steps that led us to this pot holed road in West Africa and to our growing doubts about whether the company we were on the way to visit was a worthy addition to our portfolio.

The origins of ESG

Left to their own devices, companies tend to behave badly because they take insufficient account of externalities – the incidental impact of economic activity on unrelated third parties – in their quest for value. They favour efficient solutions over responsible, fair or just solutions. The results are environmental degradation, social and economic deprivation along their supply chains, corruption and theft, and otherwise delinquent behaviour.

Efforts have been made by the suppliers of capital to rein in delinquent corporations by selective investment since at least the eighteenth century. In his sermon, 'The Use of Money', John Wesley (1703–91), a co-founder of Methodism, urged his flock to inflict no harm on their neighbours through their businesses, to avoid industries such as tanning and chemicals that can harm the health of workers and to steer clear in their investments of purveyors of 'sinful' products such as weapons, alcohol and tobacco.

Many people amassed fortunes from the slave trade before the American Civil War in 1861, but members of the Religious Society of Friends (Quakers) were not among them. They had been prohibited from participating in the slave trade since the mid-eighteenth century.

Nick Ut's Pulitzer Prize-winning photo of 9-year-old Phan Thi Kim Phuc running naked down a road, away from a village in Vietnam in June 1972, against the background of a devastating napalm bomb attack caused outrage and led to boycotts against the products of Dow Chemical, the manufacturer of napalm, and of other US companies that were doing well out of the Vietnam War.

During the widely abhorred apartheid regime in South Africa, a large number of so-called 'ethical trusts' and 'conscience funds' and scores of state and local governments adopted rules or passed laws proscribing investment in South Africa-related stocks. In July 1987, *Business Week* estimated that the total funds screened in this way were about $400 billion. According to a New York think tank, the Council on Economic Priorities, this compared with a mere $40 billion in 1984. That was an order of magnitude increase in just three years. Membership of the Social Investment Forum of fund managers tripled between 1983 and 1987.

This, and similar screening by ethical investors elsewhere in the world, put pressure on South African companies by denying them access to a significant proportion of the total global supply of business finance. It is easy to see how such pressure works. There is a sum of money, M, available to companies. A proportion of M, E, is ethically screened. Companies that pass the ethical tests have access to M, but those that do not, only have access to M–E. Other things being equal, therefore, the latter will have a higher 'cost of capital' than the former. (As we will see in Chapter 7, ESG-compliant companies enjoy a cost of capital advantage for other reasons, too. They are exposed to fewer risks and their earnings tend to be more stable.)

Eventually, a group of businesses that employed three-quarters of employed South Africans signed a charter calling for an end to apartheid. And, between 1987 and 1993, the white South African National Party held talks with the African National Congress (ANC), the anti-apartheid movement, about ending segregation and introducing majority rule. In 1990, ANC leaders, including Nelson Mandela, were released from prison. Apartheid legislation was repealed in mid-1991, paving the way for multiracial elections in April 1994.

The proscription of investments in apartheid South Africa was not, of course, the only foreign pressure on the National Party. But in helping South Africa's business community to see the light, its contribution to the multiracial democratisation of the country should not be underestimated.

The success of their anti-apartheid campaign demonstrated for the first time the power of socially responsible investors to move mountains. And this power was not relinquished after the passing of the apartheid regime.

From the mid-1990s, the attention of the responsible investor switched to 'green' issues. Environmental degradation had been of concern to young people of the baby-boomer generation since Rachel Carson's warnings about the excessive use of pesticides in her *New York Times* bestseller, *Silent Spring*, in 1962. Buckminster Fuller's polemic on the dangers of the world's dependence on fossil fuels (oil, coal and natural gas), *Operating Manual for Spaceship Earth*, appeared in 1968.

This new, planetary view of the human condition, inspired by images of the Earth from space, was echoed in the *Whole Earth Catalog* published by Stewart Brand from 1968 to 1972. It focused on self-sufficiency, ecology and the idea of 'holism' that sees everything as connected. The cover of its first edition was a colour picture of the Earth composed of several images taken in 1967 by the ATS-3 satellite.

The once-a-decade series of Earth Days, founded by US Senator Gaylord Nelson, brought together a collection of disparate single-issue pressure groups who had been fighting oil spills, polluting factories and power stations, raw sewage, toxic waste, pesticides, loss of wilderness and the extinction of wildlife. The first Earth Day in 1970 is said to have led directly to the creation of the US Environmental Protection Agency and the Clean Air, Clean Water and Endangered Species Acts.

The United Nations Conference on the Human Environment held in Stockholm in 1972 is said to have paved the way for the common approach to environmental protection that subsequently led to such agreements as the Kyoto Protocol 1997 and the Paris Accord 2016.

Another important milestone was the publication by the United Nations of *Our Common Future* in 1987, the year that Mark was asked to run the world's first emerging markets fund. Also known as the *Brundtland Report*, after former Norwegian Prime Minister Gro Harlem Brundtland, Chair of the UN's World Commission on Environment and Development, it focused on multilateralism and the interdependence of nations in achieving sustainable development. It was seen as an attempt to revive the spirit of the 1972 Stockholm Conference, and put environmental concerns firmly on the political agenda.

For a long time, 'big business' was the enemy of environmentalists. This was exemplified by Erin Brockovich, a woman with no legal training, who, in 1993, was key to putting together a case against the Pacific Gas and Electric Company of California, and won. This was famously depicted in the film, *Erin Brockovich* (2000), starring Julia Roberts.

But this enemy status was beginning to change. CERES, a network of investors, environmental organisations and other public interest groups committed to working with business to address environmental issues, was founded in 1989, by Joan Bavaria and Denis Hayes, coordinator of the first Earth Day.

The use of divestment in the anti-apartheid campaign inspired the formation of a Sudan Divestment Task Force in 2006 in response to genocide in the Darfur region, which was followed up by the passage of the US government's Sudan Accountability and Divestment Act in 2007.

After the Socially Responsible Investment (SRI) in the Rockies Conference in 2007, the rights of indigenous people in such areas as working conditions, fair wages, product safety and equal opportunity employment became a focus of SRI attention.

More recently, diversity issues, including the gender pay gap and the representation of women and ethnic and other minorities on company boards and senior executive teams, have come to the fore.

An international consolidation of SRI issues occurred in 2006, with the unveiling at the New York Stock Exchange of six UN Principles of Responsible Investment (PRIs). By August 2017, over 1,750 investors from over 50 countries, representing approximately US$70 trillion of funds under management, had signed up to the Principles.

Investors who sign up to the PRI acknowledge a duty to act in the long-term interests of beneficiaries and that environmental, social and corporate governance issues can affect portfolio performance. They recognise that applying the six UN PRI 'may better align investors with the broader objectives of society'. Where consistent with their fiduciary responsibilities, signatories will commit to the following:

1 Incorporate ESG issues into investment analysis and decision-making processes.

2 Be active owners and incorporate ESG issues into their ownership policies and practices.

3 Seek appropriate disclosure on ESG issues by the entities in which they invest.

4 Promote acceptance and implementation of the six UN PRI within the investment industry.

5 Work together to enhance their effectiveness in implementing the Principles.

6 Report on their activities and progress towards implementing the Principles.

The recent emergence of 'sustainable investing' is another consolidating SRI theme. The sustainability, or otherwise, of an investment or an investment strategy is the extent to which it can be expected to remain valid in all conceivable circumstances, over time. Shares in a company with a poor environmental record, for instance, could not be seen as a 'sustainable' investment because their value could be hit by legal action, leading to damages or by fines or other regulatory sanctions, at any time. Similarly, shares in a firm known to treat employees badly or to pay them a pittance cannot be seen as a 'sustainable' investment because their value can be reduced by low productivity, poor quality and costly labour disputes. Low corporate governance standards bring with them risks of 'agency costs' such as management incompetence and negligence, unwise or reckless decisions and strategies and illegal behaviour including fraud.

In practice, the terms 'sustainable' and 'ESG' can be treated as identical. ESG is the more precise, less equivocal term and has won the popularity contest. We shall use it throughout this book. In addition to the proscription of all forms of corruption, its 'G' component now includes investor opposition to eliminate non-voting stock, excessive executive pay, other agency costs and a lack of diversity on boards and executive committees. Other corporate sins attributed to 'G' failings include poor health and safety records, inadequate consumer protection, corruption and dishonest or unfair dealing (witness the public outrage at the revelations that German carmaker Volkswagen used so-called 'defeat devices' on its diesel engines to try to evade environmental protection regulations).

On the basis that if you have an acronym, you are going places, the recent gathering of these environmental, social and governance issues under the 'ESG' and 'sustainable investment' banners marked an important turning point in the evolution of investor power. ESG and sustainable investors are concerned, not so much with what the companies they may or may not invest in do, as with what they are.

ESG screening has become so wide-ranging and sophisticated in developed markets that it amounts to a model of what 'good' looks like, in the business world, a model which all companies are under growing pressure from ESG-sensitive investors to adopt. This is not the case in emerging markets, however.

The power of the ESG model to shape companies depends on the information on ESG-compliance available to investors. Most self-styled 'ESG investors' assume emerging-market companies to be non-compliant simply because the information they require to reach the other conclusion is not readily available.

We were making no such assumption of ESG non-compliance as we drove through the gates into the refinery complex and pulled up in front of the office block. We were sceptical because of what we had seen on the way, but our minds were open.

The state of the art

According to the Global Sustainable Investment Alliance's (GSIA) *2016: Global Sustainable Investment Review*, almost $23 trillion of assets worldwide were being 'sustainably' managed, an increase of 25 per cent since the previous 2014 biennial review. The proportion of assets said to be managed according to ESG principles increased in all regions, apart from Europe (1.1).

The review estimated that, worldwide, responsible investment accounted for 26 per cent of all professionally managed assets. The figure has fallen from 30.2 per cent in 2012, because of the decision by Sustainable Investment Forum Europe (Eurosif) to exclude certain types of ESG research from its estimate of responsibly managed assets. This has had a disproportionate impact on the global figures because Europe still accounts for more sustainably managed assets than the rest of the world put together.

Until now, the vast bulk of worldwide ESG investment (95 per cent in 2016) has been accounted for by Europe ($12 trillion in 2016), the USA ($9 trillion) and Canada ($1 trillion). Japan, Australia and New Zealand accounted for another $1 trillion between them and the rest of Asia contributed $52 billion of the $23 trillion total.

For want of reliable data, the GSIA reviews do not include any statistical information on Africa or Latin America, although there are commentaries on both of these regions in the 2016 review. The commentary on Latin America reports on the emergence of monitoring institutions in Colombia, Argentina, Chile, Mexico and Peru, often supported by local stock exchanges. The commentary on sub-Saharan Africa focuses on so-called 'impact investing' (see below) in 'the big three' economies of South Africa, Nigeria and Kenya.

The emergence of ESG and 'sustainability' as the leitmotiv of responsible investing has been accompanied by a proliferation of the ways in which such preferences are expressed. According to the GSIA, investors employ seven basic approaches:

1 *Negative/exclusionary screening*: Excluding from portfolios or funds certain sectors, companies or business practices based on ESG criteria.

2 *Positive/best-in-class screening*: Including in a portfolio or fund certain sectors, companies or projects on the basis of ESG performance, relative to industry peers.

3 *Norms-based screening*: Requiring investments to meet minimum standards of business practices, based on global norms.

4 *ESG integration*: The systematic and specific inclusion by the investment manager of ESG factors in financial analysis.

5 *Sustainability investing*: Investing in companies contributing to sustainability such as clean energy, green technology and sustainable agriculture.

6 *Impact/community investing*: Targeted investments, typically in private markets, aimed at solving social or environmental problems, and including community investing, where capital is directed to under-served individuals or communities, as well as to businesses with clear social or environmental purposes.

7 *Corporate engagement or shareholder action*: Using shareholder power to influence corporate behaviour by talking to senior management and/or boards, filing or co-filing proposals and proxy voting guided by ESG principles.

The simple 'negative-screening' investment approach accounted for the largest share of the global total, at $15.0 trillion. Next came 'ESG integration' ($10.4 trillion) and 'corporate engagement' ($8.4 trillion). The negative-screening approach accounted for the largest share in Europe. ESG integration was the lead category in the USA, Canada, Australia/New Zealand and Asia, excluding Japan. In Japan, corporate engagement dominated.

These approaches can be ranked according to how 'active' they are. The first three can be classified as essentially passive. The fourth and fifth are actively selective, and the sixth and seventh ('impact' investing and corporate engagement) are genuinely active in the sense that they use their power, as investors, to influence the objectives and behaviour of companies in their portfolios (for more on 'impact' investing, see Chapter 6).

The GSIA review shows that ESG sustainable investment is, for the most part, a Western, and specifically a European, phenomenon and that negative screening is the dominant ESG approach because it is the dominant approach in Europe. This suggests that favoured approaches to sustainable/responsible investment vary according to the maturity of local capital markets and the concerns of local populations including beneficiaries of the funds under management. For instance, the passive-screening approaches common in mature, Western markets are inapplicable in 'emerging' markets because, in these markets, too few companies pass the passive-screening tests.

For investors, this is one of the great attractions of emerging markets. In addition to offering above-average growth prospects, inefficient, badly and/or dishonestly run local companies are more remediable, by applications of shareholder power, than companies in more mature markets. There is more room for improvement. And in becoming 'better' companies, in the ESG sense, their shares become more valuable.

That is the secret of emerging markets. They reward the GSIA's 'corporate engagement' approach.

Motivations and perceptions

In adopting a 'corporate engagement' approach to ESG investment in emerging markets, we are not on a mission to spread the gospels of environmental and social responsibility and corporate governance. There may be a bit of the evangelist in us, but evangelism is not our purpose. Our purpose is to create value for those whose money we manage by finding investment opportunities in frontier areas of the world in the early stages of their economic development.

There is a hunger for economic development everywhere, in all the countries we have visited, and thus a hunger for access to the global pool of mobile capital, to which we are contributors. It is a bargain. We need their energy and creativity and their companies need our money. Their company leaders know this. They know that to attract our interest and then our money, they must comply with our ESG investment requirements.

They may think our requirements are absurd, inappropriate or plain silly, but they take them seriously and try to comply with them because to do so is a necessary condition for access to the pool of foreign capital. Some of these company leaders have returned home after studying at foreign universities and business schools. They do not think our requirements are inappropriate and they know that all the other people controlling the spigots on the pool of foreign capital do not think so either.

Many businesses in emerging markets are hungry for capital to finance growth. Since the local capital markets are still in their infancy, local supplies of capital are often limited. It is clearly in the interests of a company that is growing fast, as many are in emerging markets, to make itself attractive to foreign investors.

This hunger of companies in emerging markets for capital, and the paucity of reliable information available to foreign investors on which to make investment decisions, were brought home to Carlos in the late 1990s, soon after he had joined Mark's team.

> We were going to see the factory of a white goods company in the countryside, to the south-west of Beijing,

he recalls.

> Mark was telling me about the quality of data in China at the time. 'It is always obscure,' Mark warned. 'Don't believe anything you see or hear. It's all politicised.'
>
> We'd done some research on the company. Some of the numbers didn't really stack up, and there were some irregularities in the accounts. It was fairly obvious something was wrong. We were going to see for ourselves.
>
> When we arrived at the factory, miles from anywhere, we were greeted by a large welcoming committee of executives. They made us feel like visiting royalty. We were taken on a factory tour and I have to say, I was very impressed. Everything seemed to be running

really smoothly. They were turning out washing machines and tumble dryers like there was no tomorrow.

On the ride back to Beijing, Mark asked me what I thought of the company, after our visit. 'It's fantastic,' I replied. 'It's a great company. Everything's working. They're obviously doing very well.' Mark smiled at my youthful enthusiasm. 'I sent someone from the broking community round yesterday, to check the factory before they knew we were coming,' he told me. 'Some of those machines were in mothballs, half the rest were idle and there was hardly anyone there.' Tough competition had reduced the company's market share, and sales had suffered severely. They'd been putting on a show for us to buy time, while they fixed the sales problem.

Fast forward twenty years and things are very different. Chinese companies have to comply with governance rules now, they are rated by analysts, they have to report results on time and to publicise in English.

In just the same way as the insubstantial Chinese white goods company needed to look good for investors, it is in our interests to look attractive to potential investors in our funds, most of whom are in Europe and the USA. The GSIA's 2016 review showed that over 26 per cent of all the assets managed globally are now ESG-screened in one way or another, and of those $23 trillion or so of assets, Europe and the USA account for well over 90 per cent (see above). In our business, good ESG credentials are as valuable now as reputations for making money in emerging markets.

It does not matter what we, personally, think about the issues that are of concern to our investors. We would be no less diligent in our

ESG analysis if we were all climate change sceptics, for instance, or if we felt that low wages were better than no wages in an emerging market. The only views that matter to us and to the companies that need our money are the views of our investors and of those who may become our investors.

The views of the investors and of potential investors in our funds are important, not only because they help determine whether or not they invest. They are important also because when expressed in their roles as voters, customers, clients, suppliers or actual or prospective employees, for example, they exert influence on the contexts within which companies operate.

Environmental concerns, for instance, are not confined to the so-called 'green' political parties. They are a major and largely non-partisan theme in modern politics, which, in the Paris Accord, has produced an international agreement supposed to commit all of its signatories to meeting challenging targets for reducing carbon emissions. These commitments are likely to be expressed in local laws and regulations designed to curb carbon emissions, with which local companies will be obliged to comply.

And let us not forget that environmental issues are of concern to politicians because they are of concern to voters. Individuals also screen companies for ESG compliance at the micro level when deciding whether or not to work for them or continue to work for them, and whether or not to buy from them or continue to buy from them.

So, when we see a company that is flouting ESG principles, and seems disinclined to desist, we are unlikely to invest in it, not because it is doing wrong or behaving unethically, but because it is running various risks such as fines for breaking laws or failing to comply with regulations, industrial disputes and reductions in the company's ability to attract and keep staff and customers.

ESG funds should not be seen as 'ethical' funds that reflect the ethical prejudices of their investors in their investments. They proscribe certain practices and qualities, not because they are irresponsible, immoral or unethical per se, but because there is evidence that companies that engage in, or exhibit them, tend to underperform in capital markets.

Economic development

Entrepreneurs and the companies they form are the principal agents of economic development. To be effective agents, they need three things: a favourable business environment in which property rights and the rule of law are respected, capital and a critical mass of companies required for economic take-off.

Economic take-off can be triggered in various ways. In November 1978, an agreement was signed with thumb prints by 18 farmers of Xiaogang village in China's Anhui Province to divide the land of the local commune into household plots. The agreement was secret because such a division of communal land was illegal and punishable by death under Mao Zedong's disastrous Great Leap Forward. The contract, therefore, stipulated that if any of the signatories were beheaded or imprisoned for signing it, the other signatories would look after their children.

Xiaogang villagers were close to starvation in 1978. They had to subsist on about 50 kg of grain per head each year, not because

Xiaogang land was infertile, but because the commune's production team decided all matters relating to land and farmers had little incentive to work hard. 'All we wanted was to feed our families,' one signatory recalled. 'If we could provide enough food it was OK even if we ended up beheaded.'

In 1979, Xiaogang's grain output was 90,000 kg, about equal to the total of all its harvests in the previous 20 years. The model was copied by neighbouring villagers, and soon word of the illegal experiment reached Beijing and Mao's successor Deng Xiaoping. Instead of losing their heads, or their freedom, the 18 farmers became heroes, the experiment was officially approved and Xiaogang was dubbed 'Number One village of China's Reform'.

Surpluses replaced previously persistent shortages, and many entrepreneurial farmers used them as start-up capital for sideline businesses. By 1985, the average income of China's rural households had trebled. The dramatic increase in agricultural efficiency, and the consequent release of millions of Chinese people from the land, was the spark that ignited China's economic miracle.

It was this upsurge of entrepreneurial activity and the flood of people from the country to the towns and cities that attracted the foreign capital that financed China's industrial revolution. The seminal change, brought about by Deng's decision to endorse the revolt in Xiaogang against the collective ownership of land, was the effective ceding of property rights from central government to individuals.

That was then. This is now. China has emerged as an economic powerhouse. Other countries are emerging now, in different ways, by different routes. In each case, foreign investors are providing much of the capital required to finance the economic take-off. These investors know that no take-off occurs in a vacuum, and that each stands on the shoulders of the accumulated technologies, systems, skills and learning of those that preceded it. Today's pre-take-off countries are about to join a global, comprehensively connected economy, and will have the opportunity to leapfrog over several stages of economic development (see Chapter 6).

With the help of foreign capital, they are rapidly developing wireless and Internet protocol communications platforms. They have no need to invest in expensive landline networks. The Internet and billion-user, multipurpose platforms, such as WeChat (Tencent's so-called 'app for everything', offering messaging, social media, gaming and mobile payment), is opening up a range of new business and marketing models to entrepreneurs. Sub-Saharan African countries, in particular, are well endowed with renewable energy potential at a time when the equipment required to exploit it, including solar panels, is becoming ever cheaper. The more international mix of students at foreign universities and business schools is spreading knowledge more quickly and more widely.

In March 2018, when a protectionist trade war between the USA and China was gathering alarming momentum, 44 African countries signed a continental free trade agreement, removing tariffs on 90 per cent of imported goods. The free trade agreement could supercharge the growth rates of Africa's economies, and lead to the emergence, for the first time, of an integrated continental economy.

Due to the continent's colonial history, African countries have stronger trade links with their former colonial powers than they do with each other. The Brookings Institution estimated that, in 2016, intra-African exports made up 18 per cent of total African exports compared with 59 and 69 per cent, respectively, for intra-Asian and intra-European exports. There is, therefore, substantial scope for major expansions of intra-African trade (1.2).

If you thought that China's take-off was fast, you ain't seen nothing yet.

Our approach

By no means do all the funds that claim to be ESG-screened employ the active approaches: 'corporate engagement' and 'impact' investing. Many of them use the language of 'ESG' and 'sustainable' as little more than marketing tools. They comply with the letter of the ESG investment philosophy but not with the spirit. For them, it is a box-ticking exercise. For us, 'ESG' and 'sustainable' are more than that. They are at the core of every investment decision we take.

We suggested above that passive screening does not work in the emerging markets in which we seek investment opportunities because too few emerging market companies will pass the ESG tests. Another reason why passive screening does not work well in emerging markets is that, like early IQ tests, the ESG test is a culture-specific, one-size-fits-all test. This would not matter in an ideal world in which all national cultures were identical, and all companies were the same and competing for the same global pool of capital. In such a world, money would go to the companies that could create the most 'value', whether defined in financial or ESG terms. But in the real world, every country is different. Capital markets are not perfectly efficient and cannot be made so by asking people to jump over hurdles or tick boxes. When reliable information is hard to come by, there is no substitute for going to see for yourself.

There is another problem with box-ticking: it denies investors the opportunity to benefit from the success of companies that fail the ESG tests. Ultimately, active investors want to engage with these companies and help nudge them in different directions. They want their fund managers to take a stake in an Indonesian textile factory, for example, that does not tick any of the boxes and then help it to make good decisions and generally develop into a larger and more valuable business.

But do not get us wrong. ESG screening by tracking ESG indices may not do all that passive fund marketers claim it does, but it is much better than nothing. It helps to raise awareness of the role of investment in promoting the ESG agenda, and by putting pressure on companies to invest in technology that can reduce their carbon footprints, for example, it stimulates a general reallocation of business resources. It also encourages companies to be open about how they are dealing with their waste water and other environmental challenges, and how they are treating their employees.

To make money in emerging markets, however, you need to leave your criteria behind and go and see for yourself.

We like to hunt for investment prospects in areas or regions where hunters are thin on the ground, either because the pickings are thought to be too slim or because the big numbers on the risk side of the risk/reward ratio are too scary. We like these big numbers because we have found that corporate engagement can help to increase the reward numbers and reduce the risk numbers. But it requires a lot of work.

Once we have identified a promising investment prospect in an emerging market, we will try to find out as much as we can about its context: the situation and circumstances in which it operates. By and large, companies in emerging markets tend to be less detached from their environments than those in more mature markets. We do not mean by this that mature market companies are less sensitive to their customers. We mean they are more separate, more coherent and have fewer strings attached. In most mature markets, what you see in companies is more or less what you get. In emerging markets, in addition to what you see, you get the company's often rich and complicated ecosystem: its networks, connections, family and clan affiliations and obligations, its political allegiance if any, its competitors and allies, its friends and enemies.

The ancient Chinese networking system of *guanxi* was seen by Confucius as an important source of social stability. These days, some see it as corruption, plain and simple. But the truth is that all organisations, including companies, engage in networking, and that whether or not in a particular case it amounts to corruption, or to variants, such as nepotism and cronyism, may sometimes be a matter of opinion. To say networking is good but corruption is bad, does not get us very far because it is not always clear where one ends and the other begins. All that can be said is what Paracelsus said about mercury as a medicine: 'The poison is in the dose.'

We do desk research, of course, but we will collect most of our valuable information locally. We will do the obvious things such as talk to the company's suppliers and customers, but our main aim in our pre-investment research is to build relationships with the companies we are interested in. We track them for years and then do forensic research, with the help of former clients, former customers and former employees and associates. We also make use of our relationships with trusted local experts.

Business and financial communities in emerging markets are in many cases relatively small and the same names tend to crop up in different contexts or situations. We keep a book in which we track the careers of people of interest. If someone behaves badly in one situation we have been involved in and his or her name crops up as a director or associate of a company we are thinking of investing in, we will usually steer clear of it. This regular reappearance of bad pennies sometimes helps us to answer the fundamental question that we ask ourselves before we invest: 'Do we trust this company?'

Which brings us back to that Nigerian oil refiner, apparently being routinely robbed blind by young bandits, in cahoots with its tanker drivers.

When we arrived at the company's offices, we were greeted by a group of smartly dressed executives and given a presentation about the company that, in other circumstances, we would have found very impressive. These guys really seemed to know their business.

After the presentation, we told the managers what we had seen on the way there. I do not know what reaction we expected: shock, dismay, shame, anger? Certainly not laughter. 'That's our security system,' said their financial guy, grinning. 'It's a deal we have with the communities on the road. Depending on their size, they're allowed to tap up to 40 gallons of crude, in return for protecting the tankers from the real poachers. We ran the numbers. It's about half what we would have to pay a security firm.'

On reflection, we decided it was an unorthodox way of buying security, but effective, and appropriate in the circumstances.

2

E and S

'ESG' has become such a familiar portmanteau label for responsible investment, it is easy to forget it consists of three components.

'E' for 'environment' is based partly on: (1) an increasing consensus that climate change is caused by humans and that if we do not act now, it will be too late; (2) an aesthetic distaste for pollution and litter; (3) the threats the latter pose to public health and the wellbeing or even survival of other life forms threatened by our dirty habits, including our profligate use of resources and non-biodegradable thermoplastics. Its exhortation to companies is: 'Take a planetary view and acknowledge and make good the long-term consequences of your actions; stop acting in "unsustainable" ways; set challenging environmental goals for yourself and keep us fully informed of your progress towards them.'

Some may object to the characterisation of E as long-term and precautionary, and cite the Exxon Valdez and Deepwater Horizon oil spills as evidence of E's immediacy. Although these oil spills (in 1989 in Alaska, and 2010 in the Gulf of Mexico) aroused instant outrage and seriously damaged the environment, we see them as failures of governance rather than as evidence of environmental irresponsibility.

'S' for 'social' is based on our concern for our fellows. It is more immediate than 'E' in that it requires companies to cease and desist from cruel, exploitative and predatory treatment of people, and to contribute to the alleviation of social deprivation. In many ways, it is equivalent to Corporate Social Responsibility, but extends the domain of responsibility from the organisation and the communities in which it operates, to include the global supply chain.

'G' for 'governance' is concerned not with what a company does or does not do but with the system of rules according to which it conducts itself, and the extent to which the rules are followed. It is different from E and S in that its concerns are very specific and addressed to the board rather than the company as a whole.

For reasons we will explain later, we will focus on E and S in this chapter and discuss G in the next chapter.

Environment

Sometimes, when searching for investment opportunities in cities in central China, the sun did not penetrate the dense palls of smoke-laden air for weeks. Factory chimneys were belching out black smoke 24/7 to feed export markets ravenous for cheap Chinese goods. Air quality was not much better in the metropolitan coastal regions. Everyone on Beijing's streets wore face masks and on more than one occasion the air pollution so limited visibility that our flights from Beijing International Airport were held on the runway for several hours, waiting for the air to clear.

There seemed no help for it. Factories wanted cheap fuel, and dirty coal was the cheapest. Although clean air was in everyone's interests, it was in no individual company's interests to restrain its access to the free atmospheric dump.

It was an example of a 'tragedy of the commons', the economic concept describing how individuals, acting in their own interests, can despoil a shared resource, such as common land, the atmosphere and the oceans, to the detriment of the interests of all.

The term was coined in 1833 by the economist William Forster Lloyd, who used as an example the impact of unregulated grazing on common land ('commons'). The term was popularised in 1968 by the ecologist Garrett Hardin, who cited the atmosphere, oceans, rivers and fish stocks as examples of common natural resources threatened by unfettered use.

Well-known examples of the tragedy of the commons, also known as the 'open access problem', include the Grand Banks fishery off the coast of Newfoundland, where Rudyard Kipling's novel *Captains Courageous* (1896) was set. The Grand Banks had teemed with Atlantic cod since time immemorial, until the introduction of new fishing methods in the 1960s. The total catch soared briefly, peaked and finally plummeted. By 1990, cod had all but deserted the Grand Banks.

The so-called 'dead zones' in the world's oceans and large lakes are another example. According to the US National Oceanic and Atmospheric Administration (NOAA), they are caused by 'excessive nutrient pollution from human activities, coupled with other factors that deplete the oxygen required to support most marine life in bottom and near-bottom water' (2.1). The world's largest 'dead zone' is off the northern coast of the Gulf of Mexico. It is caused by run-off of fertiliser from farms along the Mississippi River and its tributaries.

Business economics is not concerned with externalities of this kind. ESG investors are concerned because they know that unregulated negative externalities artificially inflate profits by failing to account for the full cost of production. Companies that create such 'negative externalities' run the risk that governments will introduce laws obliging them to internalise their open access costs.

There are also positive externalities. When a company reduces its 'carbon footprint' the planet breathes a small sigh of relief, and the company becomes more attractive to ESG investors, because the value of any carbon credits it may hold rises and because the 'reputational assets' it acquires should make it easier to attract and keep customers and employees.

Public awareness of and concern about man-made environmental degradation, and their expressions in national and international regulations, agreements and commitments, such as the Paris Accord, create business opportunities for new and existing companies, such as wind turbine, solar panel and electric vehicle manufacturers.

ESG investors will be attracted by the positive externalities of these companies. Take the case of Elon Musk's electric vehicle manufacturer, Tesla Inc. It recorded a loss of almost $2 billion in 2017 and had debts of over $10 billion. Its market value touched $60 billion in the autumn of 2017, then fell on reports of production problems with its Model 3 mass-market car; however, the company was still worth $45 billion in early April 2018. The profitable General Motors, with revenues ten times Tesla's, had a market value of $52 billion on the same date.

People, particularly millennials, believe in Tesla's positive externality. For Tesla's investors, this belief contributes to the 'psychological' return on their investment, such as the feeling of being in a state of grace with the planet.

Internalising externalities

ESG investors are also attracted by technologies, systems, markets and practices that put a price on externalities.

In the old days, before thermoplastics became ubiquitous and all liquids were sold in glass bottles, you could occasionally get a little money back when you returned your 'empties': economically motivated recycling, in effect. The practice was abandoned a long time ago, for various reasons, including the emergence of the much cheaper non-biodegradable plastic bottle as the dominant handheld liquid container. We are betting that the practice will become common again.

Behind every problem lurks a business opportunity. This is no more so than in China, where high levels of air pollution in towns and cities have created mass markets for face masks and have raised public awareness of many other environmental issues.

Here is a good example. We invested in a Beijing company, with what we felt was an innovative approach to the economics of waste recycling. The company makes and operates 'reverse-vending machines' (RVMs) for polyethylene plastic bottles, widely used everywhere in the world for bottled soft drinks and water. They are a major form of litter in China's streets and public places.

The machines turn the dismal economics of 'the tragedy of the commons' upside down. People who want to dispose of their empty bottles put them in the machine and receive a payment in return. The machine compacts the bottles to prepare them for pick-up and onward transportation to recycling plants.

We thought it was a fine business model, with plenty of growth potential and good export prospects. We also thought the company, if it could attract the money it would need to grow, might make an important contribution to addressing the problem of plastic litter pollution in China (see box, below).

REVERSE-VENDING

Reverse-vending machines (RVMS) accept empties and, in exchange, return money to users. They are common in territories with mandatory recycling and container deposit laws. In some cases, bottlers pay into a central pool, from which payments are made to those who recycled their empty bottles. In other places, including Norway, the state imposes a statutory duty on suppliers to pay for their own recycling, but leaves the means by which they discharge this duty up to them. The large number of RVMs that have been installed in Norway suggests RVM systems are a cost-efficient way to discharge self-imposed or mandatory recycling obligations.

ESG investors who feel 'bullish' about the market for RVMs in the medium and long terms, as do we, on the grounds that, so far, only about 100,000 have been installed, worldwide, should do some research. They will find new RVM suppliers are cropping up all the time. Leading suppliers include Kansmacker and Envipco in the USA, Tomra in Norway, Wincor Nixdorf in Germany and Zeleno and Reverse Vending Corporation in India.

The company's 'positive externalities' – the possibility that its success would have a positive impact on the environments where it operated – was one of the reasons why it attracted our interest in the first place. We believe that in order to address 'the tragedy of the commons', it is much more effective to reward people for good behaviour than to punish them for bad behaviour with hard-to-police systems of fines or other forms of sanction.

Carbon credits

In recent years, tradable rights to emit greenhouse gases (GHGs) have been established as another form of internalising externalities. Known as 'carbon credits', these are tradable certificates or permits, endowing the holder with the right to emit a tonne of carbon dioxide (CO_2) or a tonne of the 'carbon-dioxide equivalent' of other GHGs, such as methane, nitrous oxide, hydrofluorocarbons, perfluorocarbons and sulphur hexafluoride. The credits are created by national or international agreements. GHG emissions are nominally capped by these agreements and markets are used to distribute rights to emit among a group of regulated emitters.

A company that finds it hard, or is disinclined to reduce its emissions, will sit on its credits and may even wish to buy more if the scale of its operations is growing. A company that can cut its GHG emissions, at a cost less than the market value of its carbon credits, will be motivated to sell its credits and use the proceeds to finance its emission reduction investments.

The existence of liquid-carbon credit markets that actively trade considerable volumes and assign a considerable value to rights to emit, tends to concentrate the minds of company executives on reducing emissions, and focuses the minds of other companies on developing emissions-reduction technology. The shift of focus causes an economy to reorientate itself, and devote more resources and attention to practices, technology and ways of doing business that emit less GHG or actively reduce GHG emissions. In effect, pressure on 'the commons' is eased by charging for grazing rights.

The system was formally introduced in the Kyoto Protocol of 1997 (an international agreement between more than 170 countries) and the market mechanisms were agreed through the subsequent Marrakesh Accords of 2001. The mechanisms are similar to those of the successful US Acid Rain Program, designed to cut emissions of sulphur dioxide and nitrogen oxide that combine with water to form acids. The Kyoto Protocol is an extension of the United Nations Framework Convention on Climate Change (UNFCCC) of 1992. The latter committed its state signatories to reduce GHGs, on the grounds that there was a scientific consensus that global warming was occurring and that it was predominantly 'anthropogenic', which is to say it is caused by human activity.

These commitments, accords and carbon markets are components of the global environment in which companies everywhere are formed and grow. They are the 'E' in 'ESG'. By expressing an international concern about anthropogenic climate change, they help to direct the deployment of the global pool of mobile capital.

Fans of carbon pricing, either by cap and trade systems or by simple taxation, include economist and *Financial Times* columnist, Martin Wolf. He pointed out in March 2018 that 42 national and 25 sub-national jurisdictions now put prices on carbon emissions. But 85 per cent of global emissions are not covered by carbon pricing. And even where they are, prices are well below the $40–80 per tonne of CO_2 by 2020 and \$50–100 per tonne by 2030 recommended in the report of the High-Level Commission on Carbon Prices published in 2017.

One reason for this reduced momentum of global carbon pricing is US President Donald Trump's repudiation of a commitment to cut emissions made by his predecessor's administration, on the grounds that it will damage US growth. Wolf said that this 'undermines the willingness of others to act … partly because such freeriding on their efforts is unfair, and partly because it increases the costs they have to bear, to achieve a given global outcome' (2.2).

Wolf has four proposals to make carbon pricing more effective:

1 Governments should promise to use some of the revenue from carbon pricing to lower other taxes and compensate those who spend large proportions of their income on utilities. (A case of an E/S conflict: E gains from carbon pricing are offset by S losses, for which compensation is required.)

2 Complementary moves – eliminate fossil fuel subsidies and raise regulatory standards for fuel efficiency.

3 Agree regional and, preferably, global pricing systems.

4 To prevent freeriding, impose sanctions, such as additional tariffs, on countries that refuse to play ball.

Carbon pricing works by bringing the costs of climate change forward and so making them more immediate. As active ESG investors in emerging markets, we are very much in favour of it, as long as it is recognised as a regressive tax that hits the poorest hardest and appropriate compensatory adjustments are made. By shifting resources towards cleaner technologies and renewable energy, carbon pricing, through taxation or cap and trade systems, can help emerging economies to leap-frog the dirtier, fossil-powered stages of economic emergence and at the same time create opportunities for 'green' businesses.

Social

Global supply chains – and the scrutiny to which they are routinely subjected by the press, pressure groups, national governments and international agencies, academic researchers, ratings agencies and the social media – have brought all consumers face to face with the socioeconomic provenance of what they buy.

Many have reacted to this confrontation with the consequences of their buying decisions for people in other parts of the world, with dismay and disgust that borders occasionally on outrage. They are particularly incensed by allegations of modern slavery, human trafficking and child labour. They will also withdraw their custom from companies who pay derisory wages (by their standards) and offer working conditions that range from the barely tolerable to the downright dangerous.

For example, Bangladesh's ready-made garments sector accounts for the bulk of the country's exports. It employs over 4 million people, most of whom are women and it has been estimated that its own supply chain supports a further 25 million people. The industry is of enormous importance to the economy and has played a pivotal role in the country's development.

But it is not a safe industry. On 24 April 2013, Rana Plaza, an eight-storey building housing five clothing factories in Savar near Bangladesh's capital, Dhaka, collapsed. A search-and-rescue operation lasting 17 days produced an appalling reckoning – 2,438 people had been evacuated, but more than 1,100 had died and many more had been left with life-changing injuries.

At the time, barely five months had elapsed since a fire at a seven-storey Tazreen Fashion factory near Dhaka killed 117 people, including 12 who had jumped from windows to escape the blaze. The factory made clothes for C&A, Walmart and Sears. The previous month, in Karachi, Pakistan, 254 people died and 55 were seriously injured in a fire at a four-storey factory owned by Ali Enterprises. According to the Clean Clothes Campaign (CCC), an alliance of European pressure groups seeking to improve working conditions in the global clothing industry, Ali Enterprises' workers were trapped behind barred windows and locked doors. CCC reported that: 'among the carnage and destruction also lay bundles of denim with … labels carrying German retailer KiK's brand "Okay Men"' (2.3).

Global supply chains obviously make economic sense, but their social and reputational merits are less self-evident. They are, on the contrary, repositories of potential reputational liabilities that could explode into reality at any moment, with unpredictable force. This has been clear since a gas leak from Union Carbide's Bhopal plant in India, in 1984, killed almost 20,000 people and afflicted another 500,000 with ailments such as gastrointestinal, neurological and reproductive disorders. These chances of disaster must be set against the economic benefits of such supply chains.

On the eve of the fourth anniversary of the Ali Enterprises disaster, after four years of campaigning and months of negotiations, KiK agreed to pay an additional $5.15 million in compensation for loss of earnings, medical and allied care, and rehabilitation costs to injured survivors and dependents of those killed. The negotiations between IndustriALL, CCC and KiK were facilitated by the International Labour Organization (ILO) at the request of the German Federal Ministry of Economic Cooperation and Development. Yet, on 11 September 2017, the fifth anniversary of the fire, CCC expressed its concerns about the continued lack of credible safety inspections in Pakistan's garment industry.

In 2014, a policy statement from the UK's Department for International Development (DfID) and the Foreign and Commonwealth Office after the Rana Plaza disaster (2.4) declared that: 'In line with our action plan on business and human rights, we are engaging with the government of Bangladesh and UK companies and their supply chains to . . . address key human rights risks.' It said that the UK government was focused on building safety, working conditions, communications between owners and workers, 'and urging UK buyers to take responsibility for their supply chains from the store right back to the sewing machine'.

This is the point. National governments, such as Germany's in the Ali Enterprises case and the UK's in the Rana Plaza collapse, can act as catalysts and cheerleaders for reform, but can only do so much to influence behaviour on the foreign segments of a supply chain. Ultimately, it is the buyers of manufacturing services from foreign companies who have to shoulder the main responsibility for the social consequences of their outsourcing decisions.

Governments can, however, help those with the most power over corporate behaviour, namely consumers and investors, to direct and channel their power. The California Transparency in Supply Chains Act 2010, for example, requires large retailers and manufacturers doing business in California to disclose on their websites their 'efforts to eradicate slavery and human trafficking from [their] direct supply chain for tangible goods offered for sale'. In 2015, the ILO estimated that 21 million people worldwide – 11.4 million women and girls and 9.5 million men and boys – were victims of forced labour (2.5). The UK's Modern Slavery Act 2015 requires businesses above a certain size to disclose, each year, what action they have taken to ensure there is no modern slavery in their businesses and supply chains.

Governments also use statutory reporting requirements to try to reduce trade in 'conflict resources' extracted by combatants in conflict zones and sold to finance the fighting. The most commonly mined conflict minerals are the ores of the so-called '3TG': tin, tungsten, tantalum and gold. Proceeds from the sale of 'blood' or 'conflict' diamonds are also used to finance armed conflicts. The jihadist group ISIS sold stolen oil to finance its terrorist activities in the Middle East. The US Dodd–Frank Wall Street Reform and Consumer Protection Act of 2010 required US manufacturers to audit their supply chains and report the use of conflict minerals.

Other, more subtle social issues emerge rather than burst onto the scene. The spread of the Internet in emerging markets has delivered considerable benefits: it has contributed to improving the efficiency of local companies, facilitated trade and helped to lift millions out of poverty. But it has a dark side that includes – but is not confined to – the perceived addiction of young people to computer games.

Gaming consoles made by Sony, Nintendo, Microsoft and others were banned in China in 2000 because of concern that they, and the high-definition graphical worlds they generated, were so seductive that they were having a negative impact on the mental and physical development of children.

For students of Chinese history, this triggered a strong sense of déjà vu. Concerned by the growing numbers of opium addicts in China in the early eighteenth century, the emperor prohibited the sale and smoking of opium in 1729 for all but medicinal purposes. However, having gained a monopoly of Indian opium production after its victory over the French at Plassey in 1757, the English East India Company (EEIC) identified China as a lucrative market and began to smuggle the drug into China despite the imperial prohibition.

The Qing government reaffirmed the opium prohibition in 1799 and issued a decree in 1810 that began: 'Opium has a harm. Opium is a poison, undermining our good customs and morality. Its use is prohibited by law.' The EEIC took no notice of the imperial decree and continued the illicit trade. By 1838, it was selling 1,400 tons of opium a year to China.

In March 1839, the emperor appointed Commissioner Lin Zexu to control the opium trade at the port of Canton. Lin first insisted that the imperial prohibition be respected. When the EEIC traders ignored his demand, he arrested 1,600 foreign merchants and Chinese traffickers, confiscated and then burned large quantities of the drug, and closed the port of Canton to foreign merchants. This was the *casus belli* of the First Opium War, 1839–42.

After the gaming console ban in 2000, pressure was brought to bear by the Chinese government on game developers to include anti-addiction mechanisms, also known as 'fatigue systems', that lock a player out of a game after a specified time. Even after the lifting of the gaming console ban in 2015, and the subsequent emergence of China as the world's largest and most profitable online gaming market, concerns persisted about the new opiate of the youthful masses. For example, facing criticism over the number of young Chinese players hooked on its smartphone game, *Honor of Kings*, developer Tencent introduced new rules in July 2017, limiting users under 12 to an hour of play time each day and users aged 12–18 to two hours per day.

We invested in a large online gaming company in China for a number of reasons: the market was going gangbusters, the company's business model seemed well adapted, management was impressive, the governance system was appropriate, the carbon footprint was small and, in most respects, the 'social' dimension of ESG was low risk. We knew, however, that, over the centuries, Chinese governments had demonstrated their readiness to intervene in opiate-type markets that threaten the diligence and dynamism of the labour force.

There was always a risk, therefore, of new regulations in the gaming market that could affect the business. We had enough belief in the company's adaptability to regard it as a risk worth taking.

Such risks are unavoidable, if investors want to hitch a ride on today's fastest growing markets. Concerns about game-playing addicts, breaches of data security (witness Facebook's release of user data to Cambridge Analytica in 2018), sudden revelations of a previously unsuspected technology danger (witness stories in the 1990s, which thankfully proved groundless, that aerials of mobile phones scramble brains), are ever present threats to the value of technology stocks. Who knows how much time and money today's high-technology companies will be spending 10 years from now, defending themselves against class actions relating to hitherto unsuspected health and safety dangers?

Mixtures of qualities

In practice, particular investments can never be neatly categorised as E, S or G plays, as the examples below show. We are attracted to companies with what seem to us to be potentially value-creating mixtures of qualities. The ESG qualities are becoming more important, but they do not on their own add up to a recipe for business success. Many other considerations – business ideas and models, alertness, entrepreneurialism, speed, timing, agility, knowhow, information, etc. – will also contribute to our investment decisions.

Low labour costs and a widespread command of English make the Philippines a favoured location for outsourcing business services such as call centres and account management services, particularly for US companies. These operations are typically located in high-rise buildings in Metro Manila, in such centres as the booming Fort Bonifacio. The problem is that outsourcing staff live far from the city centre, on the outskirts of Manila, and have to spend a great deal of time and money commuting by bus and car, creating pollution and congestion. It is not unusual for their journeys to work to take an hour or more. Most would like to live near to their workplace but cannot afford high apartment rents near their offices.

We have invested in a firm that develops micro-apartments to meet the demand for affordable, clean and 'hip' accommodation for young workers eager to avoid long, daily commutes or substandard informal accommodation. The micro-apartments have one-bed, two-bed and four-bed rooms, in small, efficient spaces. These developments also include facilities for recreation and meals. By reducing the need for outsourcing staff to commute during the week, our purpose-built micro-apartments not only improve the quality of their lives but also contribute to alleviating Manila's air quality and congestion problems.

Situations also arise when ESG components are in conflict. For example, we have been involved, as active investors, in restructuring programmes at recently-privatised state-owned enterprises (SoEs). As they enter the private sector, SoEs often bring a lot of baggage with them in the form of old-fashioned, inefficient processes and excessive headcounts. In many cases, high pay-roll costs had been subsidised in the state sector as a form of welfare provision, which means SoEs are often ill prepared for the rigours of competition.

A typical restructuring programme at an SoE employing 30,000 people might involve firing two-thirds of the staff. On the face of it, that is a big black mark on the social component of ESG. But consider the alternative. The SoE would not have survived in the private sector with such a huge wage bill. It would have gone bust and all 30,000 jobs would have been in jeopardy. Firing two-thirds of the staff was necessary to make the business sustainable.

And the mark on the social component is not as big or as black as it seems at first sight because heavily over-staffed SoEs are symptoms of a general structural weakness in the labour force that prevents people from moving to higher value-added employment. Mass redundancies and redeployments help to correct these weaknesses.

Another example of post-privatisation restructuring at an Eastern European SoE included generous redundancy payments and a retraining programme for those who were 'let go'. A year after it happened, Greg met, by chance, one of the 'victims' of the shake-out: a man in his early 30s, who had been a middle manager. He knew that Greg, as an active investor in the privatised SoE, had helped to push through the restructuring. But he bore him no ill will. On the contrary, 'It was the best thing that's ever happened to me,' he said. 'I started my own business with my redundancy payment, installing power supplies for cell-towers. We're doing very well.'

In 2012 the Three Gorges Dam on the Yangtze River in China became the world's largest power station, with an installed capacity of 22.5 gigawatts. It is, therefore, a big green mark for the 'E' component of ESG for the world's largest CO_2 emitter. But the mark is not as big or as green as it seems at first sight, because the dam's huge lake has inundated arable land and changed the ecology of the river valley, one consequence of which has been an increase in the incidence of landslides. There are also some black marks on the S component of ESG in the form of 1.3 million people displaced by the lake and the flooding of archaeological and cultural sites.

A few years ago, Mark visited Nine Dragons Paper Holdings. 'I sat down with this lady and her husband,' he recalled, 'and started talking to him. She immediately held up a hand to stop me. "I run this company," she said.' This was executive chairwoman Zhang Yin, one of China's richest women. She founded the company in 1995, and built it up into Asia's largest paperboard producer:

> We went into the factory. You could eat off the floor, it was so clean. And what was she doing? Importing waste cartons from North America and converting them into paper cartons again. When they import the cartons, there may be some wire or plastic fasteners they have to dig out. She took me to a little garden by the river. There were some odd-looking chairs, made of a composite of the waste wire and plastic fasteners and epoxy. They recycled everything. She was solving America's waste-paperboard problem by importing it and converting it into useful material, some of which was then used to export goods to the US.

Nine Dragons scores well on the 'E' dimension of ESG because recycling is an integral part of 'E'. Most paper mills use forest products for paper production. Nine Dragons uses recycled paper as its raw material and recycles over 10 million tonnes of fibre each year. But it does not score so well on the 'S' dimension. In April 2008, Students and Scholars Against Corporate Misbehaviour (SACOM), a millennial-generation pressure group based in Hong Kong, issued a report of an investigation of Nine Dragons, accusing the company of unethical labour practices. It published the *Nine Dragons Paper Employee Handbook*, which contained numerous rules and details of a system of employee fines that was heavily criticised. Nine Dragons subsequently ceased to impose worker fines.

As we shall see in Chapter 7, these mixtures of ESG qualities pose 'impact' measurement challenges. In the long run, it will not be enough to measure 'positive' impact. We will also have to measure 'negative' impact, subtract the latter from the former and end up with a company's 'net-positive' impact.

Investors

Norway's Government Pension Fund Global, commonly known as the Oil Fund or Norges, was created in 1990 to invest surplus revenue from the Norwegian petroleum sector. It has over $1 trillion in assets and owns 1.3 per cent of all stocks and shares traded worldwide, making it the world's largest sovereign wealth fund. As of September 2017, it was worth $192,307 per Norwegian citizen.

An Advisory Council on Ethics for the fund was established by royal decree in November 2004, and ethical guidelines were issued by Norway's Ministry of Finance. These bar the fund from investing in companies that directly or indirectly contribute to killing and torture, the deprivation of freedom and other violations of human rights in conflicts. The fund's Council on Ethics is aided by RepRisk ESG Business Intelligence, a research firm that provides ESG risk data. RepRisk monitors the companies in the fund's portfolio for issues such as human rights violations, including child labour, forced labour and violations of individual rights in conflict areas, corruption and gross environmental degradation.

In July 2018, Norges announced that it had sold its bonds of US utility, PacifiCorp, and had placed its parent Warren Buffett's Berkshire Hathaway Energy, and another utility company MidAmerican Energy, 'under observation' because they use coal. It was part of the fund's purging of its fixed-income portfolio of companies that derive more than 30 per cent of their business from coal.

Norges also announced the disposal of its holding in JBS, the world's largest meatpacker, which has been at the centre of a major corruption scandal in Brazil, said to involve payment of bribes to 1,800 politicians over several years. The oil fund also decided to exclude Luthai Textile, a Chinese owner of clothes factories, for human rights violations; to place Nien Hsing Textile, a Taiwanese company, 'under observation' for the same reason; and to keep an eye, through its 'active ownership' process, on the Indian chemicals group UPL's promise to end its use of child labour (2.6).

Most of the world's largest megafunds, including the Japanese government's $1.3 trillion pension fund, the $564 billion Dutch pension fund manager APG and Germany's Union Asset Management with $402 billion under management, have declared for ESG in one way or another.

Another megafund, the California Public Employees' Retirement System (CalPERS), with $344 billion under management, says it wants its portfolio companies to have 'healthy, productive and motivated workforces ... This is why we care about labour practices and health and safety standards. We have seen ... when companies don't consider the well-being of their employees, they risk potential litigation, their reputations and their ability to operate.' CalPERS addresses social issues through proxy voting and shareholder campaigns. It also engages with portfolio companies directly on important social issues, such as fair labour practices in supply chains, health and safety and human rights.

Opportunities

As with all components of the ESG triptych, there are opportunities to grasp as well as problems to solve in the social component.

Humanity United – supported by the self-styled 'philanthropic investment firm' set up in 2004 by eBay founder, Pierre Omidyar, and his wife, Pam – has raised $23 million to invest in technology start-up companies committed to fighting human trafficking, forced labour and other human rights violations in global supply chains. The new fund, called Working Capital, says it has the support of the Walmart Foundation, C&A Foundation, Stardust Equity and The Walt Disney Company (2.7).

The fund's target areas include product traceability, worker engagement, sourcing platforms, risk assessment and more ethical recruiting tools. The technologies that Working Capital portfolio companies may be working with include blockchain, artificial intelligence, digital identity, machine learning and the so-called 'Internet of Things'.

In areas of the world where the exploitation of workers and a cavalier attitude to workplace health and safety are commonplace, notable exceptions are attractive to foreign investors. We found a very interesting company in Jakarta, the capital city of Indonesia, that makes motor scooters. Amid all the sweatshops and rickety, high-rise factories, its treatment of employees stands out. Every worker has health insurance, there is a clinic on-site and there is staff accommodation. That is why people want to work there. It is a space where they can have a life. It may seem a little old-fashioned to Western eyes – like the Cadbury chocolate dynasty in England, with its Quaker beliefs and model village for employees – but it is a quality that could take it a long way in an increasingly curious, transparent, ESG-sensitive world.

Another way of transforming the visceral disgust of consumers and investors with exploitative and predatory employment practices is to differentiate the products of 'good' and 'bad' employers, in this sense, in the marketplace. Labels such as the Fairtrade logo do this by adding non-financial value to a commodity product from a certified 'good' employer for which socially sensitive consumers are willing to pay a premium (see p. 192).

The bubble reputation

Of the three dimensions of ESG, 'S' is the most conspicuous. Issues to do with 'E' unfold at a glacial pace, so to speak. Issues to do with 'G' usually operate behind the scenes, out of the public eye. But issues to do with 'S' are 'in your face' – often brutal, sometimes bloody and occasionally absolutely appalling. They get people out on the streets: witness the rallies and protests against retailers that purchase from companies and sites where disasters occur, and they have 'news values' that make the headlines.

In fact, the impact of 'S' issues on ostensibly implicated companies can be out of all proportion to the incidents concerned. This problem was highlighted in the summer of 2010 by a story made much of in the press: an apparent suicide 'cluster' at the 400,000-employee Shenzhen factory of Foxconn Technology Group. Taiwan-based Foxconn employed 930,000 people worldwide in 2010. It was the world's largest contract electronics manufacturer and counted Apple, Dell, Hewlett-Packard, Nokia, Sony and Nintendo among its clients.

The inference was that working conditions and pay at 'Foxconn City', as the site is known, and at other Foxconn sites in mainland China, were so awful that their desperate employees were being driven to take their own lives. But *The Economist* later pointed out that, although the number of workplace suicides at Foxconn seemed large, the suicide rate in Foxconn City was actually lower than China's overall suicide rate (2.8). Others said this was true but misleading because it failed to note that 44 per cent of China's suicides were aged 65 or over and 79 per cent lived in rural areas.

Still others could not see what the fuss was about. Boy Lüthje of Germany's Institute of Social Research told *The Economist* that Foxconn treated its employees quite well by Chinese standards. It paid a minimum monthly wage of 900 yuan ($130), and provided free recreational facilities, food and lodging at some of its sites.

Whatever the truth of the matter, the story clearly pushed the 'S' alert button. Soon after the suicide story broke, Foxconn's chairman, Terry Gou, announced an increase in minimum pay to 1,200 yuan a month at Foxconn's Chinese plants and, a week later, promised another rise in October to 2,000 yuan a month at the Foxconn City complex in Shenzhen.

Apple was also sensitive to the potential reputational damage of the story. At a live question-and-answer session during the D8 technology conference in California in June 2010, chief executive officer (CEO) Steve Jobs said, 'Apple is extraordinarily diligent and rigorous about vetting its manufacturing partners. Foxconn isn't a sweatshop. They've got restaurants and swimming pools … For a factory, it's a pretty nice factory.' He observed that the Foxconn suicide rate was below the national average in the US. 'But this is very troubling to us,' he added. 'So we send over our own people, and some outside folks as well, to look into the issue' (2.9).

This episode illustrates the fragility of corporate and brand reputations, their sensitivity to unexpected events and capricious news values, and the insistence of many ordinary people, including their existing and prospective customers and employees, that firms take responsibility, not only for their own actions, but for those of the rest of their supply chains, too.

ES & G

In ESG debates, our basic position is similar to Paul the Apostle's in his Epistle to the Corinthians: 'And now abideth environment, society, governance, these three; but the foremost of these is governance.' We believe that a sensitivity to the environment and society is an essential part of good management, and ensuring good management is an essential objective of corporate governance. This says nothing about the relative importance of E, S and G, of course. It simply recognises the direction of cause and effect.

Without good governance, companies with no monopoly or state subsidy will tend to stumble from crisis to crisis and expire. With good governance, they comply with popular concerns about the environment and the socioeconomic aspects of global supply chains and grow steadily. But they do not grow because they are sensitive to the environment and the socioeconomic aspects of global supply chains. They grow because growth and good management are both the creatures of good corporate governance.

The other reason we, as active investors, see G as the *primus inter pares* in the ESG scheme of things is that it is our way into the company. Investors exert their power, as owners, through a set of rules and associated rights and responsibilities that make up the governance system. We sometimes try to persuade boards to tune or modify their governance systems, but there must be a system. A management team that shows no signs of respecting the rights of all investors or of abiding by the rules of governance would find it extremely hard to attract new capital.

3

Governance

With substantial hydroelectric power, and among the largest oil and gas reserves in Europe, Romania is the most energy self-sufficient European Union (EU) member state. A few years ago, an Austrian oil and gas company, in which we had invested, began negotiating to buy a Romanian oil-refining business. Due diligence had revealed a mixed picture. The company seemed to be potentially very profitable, but there were some puzzling anomalies in the numbers, particularly in the relationship between fluid input and output volumes.

The opacity of the numbers created risks, but we were used to that. The business model appeared sound and growth prospects were thought to be good enough to offset the risk. The Austrian company decided to take the plunge and acquired a controlling interest in the Romanian refiner.

However, it took some precautions. Suspecting that skulduggery of some kind would turn out to be the cause of the anomalous numbers, the Austrian company hired an East German anti-corruption agent, a former spy for East Germany's secret police, the Stasi. He found hundreds of pipes leading from the plant's output pipelines into the forest on the other side of the refinery's boundary fence. Through these parasitical pipelines, refined product was being stolen for subsequent sale on the black market.

It would have been difficult and very expensive to send plant and people into the forest to rip them all up, so the problem was solved by the simple expedient of closing the pipeline temporarily and pumping concrete slurry down the illegal spur lines.

Later, the anti-corruption investigator discovered toxic waste from the refinery had been illegally buried on a nearby strip of land. The new Austrian parent company announced the discovery to the local press and immediately embarked on a $100 million remediation of the contaminated area.

The acquisition of a local business by a foreign company, and subsequent revelations of corruption and illegal disposal of toxic waste in open countryside, would usually generate storms of protest and hostile press coverage about predatory invaders. In this case, the conventional storyline was turned on its head. The foreign acquirer had stamped out corruption, and had discovered and cleaned up contaminated land. The positive press coverage that followed was given added retro glamour by the role played by a former communist spy from East Germany.

In Chapter 4, there is also the example of a company we recently invested in, the Romanian state-controlled utility, Hidroelectrica, which, unaccountably for a hydroelectric generating company with negligible marginal costs, had been losing money.

Our purpose in telling these stories is not to suggest that Romania is a conspicuously corrupt country (it is not, see below), but to show how corrupt practices and delinquent or non-existent corporate governance offer opportunities for investors. If you are able and willing to engage with local managers and officials, and have a good understanding of the strengths and weaknesses of local institutions, you can make money by investing in a company plagued by corrupt practices and returning it to the straight and narrow.

Mapping corruption

Corruption is a venal form of national and company governance that impoverishes society. It is more common in some countries and some companies than in others, but that is not because the people of some countries are more corrupt than those of others. It is because, in countries where institutions such as property rights and the rule of law are weak or non-existent, corruption becomes rampant at the top and, consequently, a way of life in many other businesses. As the Sudanese-born philanthropist, Mo Ibrahim, put it when talking about his Ibrahim Prize for Achievement in African Leadership: 'It is the head of the fish that goes rotten first, so what's needed is to shed a light on the performance of the leadership' (3.1).

In Transparency International's Corruption Perceptions Index (CPI) in 2017, Romania ranked 59 out of a total of 180 countries. Table 3.1 lists the top (least corrupt) and bottom (most corrupt) countries in the years 2013–17, according to their CPI scores, and includes, in the two right-hand columns, the IMF's estimates of gross domestic product (GDP) per capita of population in 2017, at Purchasing Power Parity, and each country's GDP/capita ranking.

Correlation does not necessarily mean causation, but the clear link in these figures between high levels of corruption and low levels of

Table 3.1 *The good, the bad and the ugly*

CPI Rank	Country	2017	2016	2015	2014	2013	GDP/ capita (Int$K)*	Rank (IMF)
1	New Zealand	89	90	91	91	91	38.5	31
2	Denmark	88	90	91	92	91	49.6	20
3=	Finland	85	89	90	89	89	44.0	25
3=	Norway	85	85	88	86	86	70.6	6
3=	Switzerland	85	86	86	86	85	61.4	9
6=	Singapore	84	84	85	84	86	90.5	3
6=	Sweden	84	88	89	87	89	51.3	16
8=	Canada	82	82	83	81	81	48.1	22
8=	Luxembourg	82	81	85	82	80	109.2	2
8=	Netherlands	82	83	84	83	83	53.6	13
8=	UK	82	81	81	78	76	43.6	26
12	Germany	81	81	81	79	78	50.2	17
...								
169	Venezuela	18	17	17	19	20	12.4	96
171=	Equatorial Guinea	17	N/A	N/A	N/A	N/A	34.9	37
171=	Guinea-Bissau	17	16	17	19	19	1.8	173
171=	North Korea	17	12	8	8	8	N/A	N/A
171=	Libya	17	14	16	18	15	9.8	108
175=	Sudan	16	14	12	11	11	4.6	138
175=	Yemen	16	14	18	19	18	2.3	161
177	Afghanistan	15	15	11	12	8	1.9	170
178	Syria	14	13	18	20	17	N/A	N/A

179	South Sudan	12	11	15	15	14	1.5	176
180	Somalia	9	10	8	8	8	N/A	N/A

Rankings of other selected countries

13	Australia	77	79	79	80	81	49.9	18
16	USA	75	74	76	74	73	59.5	11
20	Japan	73	72	75	76	74	42.7	28
23	France	70	69	70	69	71	43.6	27
29	Portugal	63	62	64	63	62	30.3	43
32	Israel	62	64	61	60	61	36.3	35
34	Botswana	61	60	63	63	64	18.1	71
42	Spain	57	58	58	60	59	38.2	32
46	Georgia	56	57	52	52	49	10.6	105
51	South Korea	54	53	54	55	55	39.4	30
54	Italy	50	47	44	43	43	38.0	33
57	Saudi Arabia	46	46	52	49	46	55.3	12
59=	Greece	48	44	46	43	40	27.8	49
59=	Romania	48	48	46	45	43	24.0	59
66	Hungary	45	48	51	54	54	28.9	45
68	Belarus	44	40	32	31	29	18.6	70
71	South Africa	43	45	44	44	42	13.4	89
77	China	41	40	37	36	40	16.6	79
81=	India	40	40	38	38	36	7.2	122
81=	Turkey	40	41	42	45	50	26.5	53
85	Argentina	39	36	32	34	34	20.7	63

(Continued)

Table 3.1 *Continued*

CPI Rank	Country	2017	2016	2015	2014	2013	GDP/ capita (Int$K)*	Rank (IMF)
96=	Brazil	37	40	38	43	42	15.5	81
96=	Indonesia	37	37	36	34	32	12.4	97
111	Philippines	34	35	35	38	36	8.2	118
117=	Egypt	32	34	36	37	32	13.0	92
117=	Pakistan	32	32	30	29	28	5.4	135
130=	Iran	30	29	27	27	25	20.0	64
130=	Ukraine	30	29	27	26	25	8.7	114
135=	Mexico	29	30	31	35	34	19.5	65
135=	Russia	29	29	29	27	28	27.9	48
143	Kenya	28	26	25	25	27	3.5	149
148	Nigeria	27	28	26	27	25	5.9	129

Note: * Geary–Khamis or International dollars (000s)
Sources: Transparency International and International Monetary Fund.

GDP per head strongly suggests that corruption is a very bad form of governance that impoverishes societies. It substitutes inefficient systems of patronage for free markets, leads to a suboptimal allocation of resources and consequently to low returns on investment and equity. And, worst of all, corruption suppresses the entrepreneurial energy that drives economic growth, by denying the rights of local entrepreneurs to the wealth they create. If people believe businesses they build will be stolen by corrupt officials or by predatory conglomerates, they will not seek out entrepreneurial opportunities.

This link between corruption and poverty is probably stronger than the figures suggest, for two reasons: first, because a number of highly corrupt countries, including Russia and Venezuela, are rich in natural resources such as oil and gas, which inflates GDP; second, because the distribution of GDP is invariably very unequal in corrupt societies.

As José Ugaz, Chair of Transparency International, puts it on the Transparency International website: 'In too many countries, people are deprived of their most basic needs and go to bed hungry every night, because of corruption, while the powerful and corrupt enjoy lavish lifestyles with impunity.'

A high degree of inequality in a country will deter a foreign investor because inequality leads to social and political unrest. The country becomes vulnerable to coups and populist leaders who call on the people to rise up against and throw out their corrupt or incompetent governments. There may be calls for nationalisation of foreign-owned businesses without compensation, increases in tax rates, the introduction of crippling regulatory regimes, etc. The message for investors is to stay well clear of countries where wealth is distributed very unequally.

Inequality is usually measured by the Gini coefficient, which ranges from 0 (perfect equality) to 1 (one person owns all the wealth). The US Central Intelligence Agency (CIA) is interested in Gini coefficients because high Ginis are good predictors of civil unrest.

The riskiness of countries with high levels of corruption and economic inequality means corrupt regimes are inherently fragile. Their inability to attract foreign direct investment restrains the levels of economic activity well below these countries' potentials and puts their governments under pressure to reform themselves.

Announcements of 'anti-corruption' policies by incumbents, or political parties aiming to replace them, are designed as much to attract more foreign investment as to appease angry electorates. Some turn out to have more substance than others, but, over time, changes in Transparency International's CPI rankings show that no country is irredeemably corrupt.

CPI scores change constantly and suggesting that perceptions of corruption are affected by particular events. The UK's 6-point rise between 2013 and 2017 may be a recovery from the effects of the LIBOR fixing scandal in the wake of the 2007–2008 financial crisis. Greece's 8-point improvement over the period may reflect a perceived tightening of the country's governance after the Greek debt crisis that began in 2009. Turkey's vertiginous 10-point fall in its perceived corruption score probably has a lot to do with the political turbulence in the country.

It is not surprising that most CPI movements are modest. Once established, corrupt national governance systems, and the corrupted cultures they breed, become normal and unremarkable. When gathering up his things at the end of a meeting with officials of a state-controlled company in Moscow, Mark found his mobile phone was missing. The security staff were dismayed. They searched high and low for the phone, but to no avail. When he returned to the same building a few years later, the security staff told him, 'We're still looking for your phone.' He thought no more about it. It was par for the course. Quite unremarkable.

Corruption, fraud and outright theft might seem endemic in some emerging markets, but they are not incorrigible. There is always pressure for reform. We hope by actively engaging on these issues we may be contributing to improvements in corporate governance in emerging markets. Perhaps the revelations of skulduggery at the Romanian refinery described at the beginning of the chapter were partly responsible for a 5-point improvement in Romania's CPI score between 2013 and 2017.

Step by step. Too many powerful people have vested interests in the status quo for governance reform to be easy. It takes time for good governance to drive out bad governance even when it is clear that the economic benefits of the process for the population at large are likely to be enormous.

The quality of governance

Corruption, fraud, theft and other forms of criminality are not the only corporate governance failings of concern to investors. Agency costs – the costs of hiring others to run your business – include: incompetence; negligence; recklessness; conflicts of interests and conflicts of interest and duty; a lack of transparency; unfair and unequal treatment of shareholders; insufficient separation of the powers of the executive committee and the board; and insufficiently diverse boards in which so-called 'group think' is an ever-present danger.

Chuck Prince, the former CEO of Citigroup, illustrated the dangerous power of 'group think' when he explained Citi's ill-fated enthusiasm for subprime mortgages and consumer loans in July 2007 in the *Financial Times*: 'as long as the music is playing, you've got to get up and dance'. Four months later, Prince resigned after Citigroup announced a fourth-quarter loss of almost $10 billion.

After the chastening lessons learned by mature Western economies in the 2007–2008 financial crisis, everyone knows, or can find out, what 'good' corporate governance looks like. The reasons why some listed companies do not comply with corporate governance codes vary from the wish of founders to retain control, the determination of ambitious CEOs not to be hamstrung by their boards, the resistance of those with vested interests in weak controls and oversight, and government interference, to inertia, a general lack of pressure to comply and sheer laziness.

A few years ago, we flew to Ankara for a meeting with the CEO of Turkish Airlines. We were thinking of investing in the company, alongside the Turkish government, which still held a controlling interest. To be frank, we were not optimistic. Turkey was not known for its high standards of corporate governance and we knew all too well about the risks of being a minority shareholder in a company controlled by a government. But we were interested to hear how far the company would go to accommodate our governance demands.

When we asked if we could have an independent director on the board, the CEO said we would have to talk to the government. Not a good sign. It was up to the board, not the largest shareholder, to nominate a new director. But we had nothing to lose. We decided to go along with the CEO's suggestion and arranged a meeting with the Minister of Finance. We arrived at the ministry offices at the appointed time and then had to go through a seemingly interminable series of security checks. We were eventually ushered into a plush office. The minister stood up, greeted us and gestured towards two leather chairs.

After the usual pleasantries and assurances by our host that foreign investors were welcome in Turkey, we asked the minister the same question we had asked the CEO, knowing the answer could only be a polite, but firm, 'No.' We asked, 'If we invest in Turkish Airlines, can we have an independent director on the board?'

'Why only one?' was the astonishing reply. 'Why not two?'

The lesson here is: 'Don't jump to conclusions about corporate governance.' The Turkish government was more pragmatic and market-orientated than it appeared. There was a willingness to modernise the Turkish Airlines board by appointing independent directors. It had not happened because no one had been pushing for reform. This demonstrates the value of shareholder engagement and advocacy at a time when the general trend is towards passive investment.

It also illustrates the influence that foreign investors as a group have on governments of countries such as Turkey that need large inflows of foreign capital to finance large trade deficits. At the time of writing, Turkey's structural current account deficit is running at close to 6 per cent of GDP.

Governance and gender

Last, but not least, good governance includes paying attention to the issue of diversity, particularly the representation of women in business, government and all institutions. Like many other areas of human endeavour, the moral questions really point to the most beneficial outcomes for mankind. Fully including women means adding enormous intellectual, creative and productive assets to all manner of enterprise.

The recognition of the importance of gender equality is not new: the 1979 United Nations Convention on the Elimination of All Forms of Discrimination Against Women (CEDAW) has been ratified by 187 countries. And, in 2010, the United Nations General Assembly created UN Women to accelerate progress on gender equality and women's empowerment. But it is only in recent years that this area is finally receiving the wider attention it deserves.

However, there is still some way to go. Large gender wage gaps exist in countries at all levels of GDP per capita (3.2). According to the World Economic Forum's *Global Gender Gap Report 2018*, worldwide, there remains a 32 per cent average gender gap to be closed (3.3). Women represent 4.8 per cent of CEOs in the US Fortune 500 companies, 5.6 per cent in China's publicly listed companies, 1.8 per cent in Latin 500 companies, 2.8 per cent in publicly traded companies in the EU, 3 per cent among the Mexico Expansion 300 companies and 4 per cent of CEOs among India's Mumbai Stock Exchange 100 companies (3.4).

Gender equality and the rights of minorities are not only a moral imperative but make economic sense. It is important to consider all talents in society. And, clearly, if we are focusing on fostering the talents of men while neglecting those of women, we are missing at least half of all available brainpower, creativity and abilities. Therefore, it would be a severe oversight and a loss to a society as well as to corporates.

Some recent studies have started to throw some light on how much of an economic loss this causes: in 2015, the McKinsey Global Institute (MGI) (3.5) estimated that a scenario in which women achieved complete gender parity with men could increase global output by more than one-quarter relative to a business-as-usual scenario. Similarly, according to research carried out in 2016 by PricewaterhouseCoopers (PwC) (3.6), reducing the gender pay gap and increasing female employment rates across Organisation for Economic Co-operation and Development's (OECD) countries to match Sweden's – which has one of the highest female employment rates within the OECD – could boost GDP product by $6 trillion. The gains would come from increased female participation in the labour market, entrepreneurship and women moving into higher-paid and skilled jobs.

On the micro-level, an analysis by the Peterson Institute of Global Economics (3.7) of a global survey of 21,980 firms from 91 countries suggests that the presence of women in corporate leadership positions may improve firm performance. This correlation could reflect either the pay-off to non-discrimination or the fact that women increase a firm's skill diversity. Either way, as a whole, firms and society benefit from a stronger participation of women in the labour market. Similar effects can be seen where ethnic and cultural minorities have a stronger representation in corporate leadership positions (3.8).

Interestingly, according to the *Global Gender Gap Report 2018* (3.9), which considers women's political empowerment, economic participation, health and educational attainment, women in some emerging economies are joining the top ranks of business management at the same pace as those in developed countries. In the top ten countries of the Global Gender Gap Index are Nicaragua (5), Rwanda (6), the Philippines (8) and Namibia (10). The UK ranks 15 and the USA 51.

However, in our work in the small and mid-cap sector in emerging markets, we often find that the awareness of gender issues and understanding of the positive effect of a stronger and more equal female participation in the work force is still lacking. This offers another important opportunity for ESG-conscious investors to create value as well as positive impact.

In Vietnam, for example, we invested in the largest producer of milk products. The company had been a state enterprise and was privatised in the early 2000s. A woman, who had joined the company as an engineer in the 1970s, was placed in the leadership position. She was able to transform this sleepy bureaucratic state-owed enterprise into one of the most successful firms in the country. Meanwhile, Forbes listed her as one of the 50 most influential businesswomen in Asia.

Closing the circle, women feel much stronger about the social impact of their investments than men do. Women across all age cohorts show overwhelming interest in socially responsible and impact investing as compared to men (70–79 per cent of women show interest versus 28–62 per cent of men, depending on the study) (3.10). One could almost surmise that the trend towards stronger and more equal participation of women in the labour market would go hand in hand with a continued drive of assets in the direction of sustainable investments.

Influencing governance

Passive investors must endure poor corporate governance. They have surrendered their power to change it. Active, human investors can have a major impact on a company. They gather knowledge about the company, they can apply pressure for reform and they can help to ensure compliance with corporate governance standards. They ask the vital question that never crosses the mind of an administrator of a tracker fund, 'Do we trust this company?'

Human, but not algorithmic, investors will also use their own networks, including other companies they have invested in, to help new portfolio companies. Turkish Airlines won plaudits for its in-flight meals after it subcontracted its catering to a restaurant company in Vienna we had recommended.

We believe independent non-executive directors have a crucial role to play in maintaining corporate governance standards, but we recognise that, in some markets, they are not easy to find. We were an investor in a now defunct Latin American department store chain for many years. One day, the chief financial officer (CFO) left and assets turned out to be missing. We decided to take legal action, and arranged a meeting with the new director of the national stock market regulator (the equivalent of the US Securities and Exchange Commission) to discuss the case. Imagine our surprise when the new director turned out to be the retailer's missing CFO.

When the local pool of qualified directors is small, conflicts of interest and the need to avoid any accusations of cronyism or nepotism may make it hard to assemble a balanced board, capable of carrying out its independent oversight duties.

Moreover, it is not enough to have a balanced board and agreed rules of governance and delegation frameworks. They will count for nothing, if those who should feel bound by the rules regard them as window dressing and fail to comply with them.

We invested in a large Mexican retailer, partly because of its high corporate governance standards: they were transparent and the executives played by the rules. Then, one day, a pair of investment bankers flew in from Wall Street and dazzled the company's finance director with visions of the profits the retailer could make from the 'super peso', as Mexico's currency was being characterised in the press in 2008. The CFO was persuaded and exposed the company to a huge, off-balance-sheet currency risk by taking a speculative position in currency derivatives with escalating pay-off structures that allowed losses to accumulate rapidly.

Derivatives are useful in hedging against currency risks, but this was a gamble, plain and simple. It would have produced a huge profit if the peso had remained 'super'. It did not. It went in the opposite direction, fast. The company, which was very profitable, filed for bankruptcy a few months later, with losses approaching $2 billion. There was a lesson here. The company's governance system was good, by Mexican standards, but the CFO did not feel it obliged him to be prudent.

Business and politics

An investor in emerging markets cannot go far without encountering the national government in some form or another as the controlling shareholder, regulator, customer, landlord, grant- or subsidy-giver, main competitor or sponsor of 'national champion' companies. Business and politics are often intertwined in a variety of overt and subtle ways, all of which investors must try to understand and take into account when making an investment decision.

It is taken for granted in the West that governments lack the skills, flexibility and speed of decision-making needed to succeed in the private sector, and that all state-owned enterprises should, therefore, be 'privatised'.

Elsewhere, state ownership of the 'commanding heights' of the economy continues to be seen as an essential instrument of policy. But cracks are appearing in these command economy bastions, as the likes of Saudi Aramco, the Kingdom of Saudi Arabia's state-owned oil company, seek to raise money on international capital markets. Following what appeared to be a disagreement between King Salman and his heir, Mohammed bin Salman, the kingdom's plan to raise an estimated $100 billion through an initial public offering (IPO) of 5 per cent of Saudi Aramco was officially postponed in August 2018.

It was not abandoned, however. If and when it goes ahead, the shares would be listed initially on the kingdom's Tadawul exchange, and there was talk before the postponement of subsequent listings abroad such as in London, New York or Hong Kong (3.11).

In preparation for the IPO, which will require the support of foreign investors to succeed, Saudi Arabia had enacted reforms to allow foreign investors to participate in local IPOs and to align its securities regulations to international standards. The reforms included the appointment in April 2018 of five new board members, including Peter Cella, CEO of Chevron Philips Chemical, former CEO of Sunoco, Lynn Elsenhans, and soon to be former CEO of DowDuPont, Andrew Liveris, plus new corporate governance rules protecting the rights of minority shareholders.

Issues of such small fractions of the equity cede no power to new minority shareholders, but potential investors are unlikely to subscribe for shares if they believe the controlling shareholders will take no account of their interests. They need to be confident that the company will comply with generally accepted standards of corporate governance, particularly with regard to the treatment of minority shareholders.

The judgement of the international financial community before the postponement was that Saudi Arabia was making the right noises. The FTSE Russell index had said it was planning a staged inclusion of Saudi equities in its emerging markets index beginning in March 2019, and it was looking as if MSCI's emerging markets index would follow suit. The inclusion of Saudi equities in such indices would transform the local market because it would lead to the inflow of billions of dollars from passive funds.

Some years ago, we acquired shares in Aluminum Corporation of China Ltd (Chalco). The company was listed on the New York, Hong Kong and Shanghai stock exchanges, but was still majority owned by state-owned Aluminum Corporation of China (Chinalco). At first, Chalco's corporate governance system, particularly its treatment of minority shareholders, left a lot to be desired. That changed later, when the Chinese government issued a proclamation requiring its state-owned enterprises to get their corporate governance acts together.

Soon afterwards, Mark was invited to Beijing to meet Chalco's chairman. 'We sat at a table in a large room,' he recalls, 'and the chairman stood up to address us. "Before we begin," he said, "I want to apologise. We've treated our [minority] shareholders badly. Our corporate governance has been poor. We're going to improve."'

When the SoEs of command economies dip their toes into global capital markets with IPOs, it may be their first encounter with the ideas of corporate governance: the need to recognise the rights of minority shareholders, and the importance of accurate and timely reporting. It is a nightmare for corrupt managers and officials, of course, but for their more honest and responsible colleagues, there is little to object to in the principles, rules and frameworks of modern corporate governance. They simply have not previously given such issues much thought. Which is not to say that powerful and politically influential actors don't have substantial vested interests in the status quo.

Chaebol under siege

The *chaebol* – from *jae* (wealth or property) and *beol* (faction or clan) – are the conglomerates that have dominated South Korea's economy since the early 1960s. There are two dozen or so chaebol, the best known of which, outside South Korea, are Samsung, Hyundai and LG (Lucky Goldstar). Modelled to some extent on the Japanese business federations known as *zaibatsu*, they are family-controlled and politically connected.

The dynastic nature of chaebol is derived from the principles of Confucianism and the role hierarchy plays in the maintenance of stability. This produces the four principles of *ren* (benevolence), *yi* (propriety), *xiao* (filial piety) and *zhong* (loyalty). Family plays a central role in Confucian thought, from the basic level of parents and their children, to the state and its citizens, and the chief executive and his or her employees.

Historically, the chaebol have also played an active role in South Korean politics. In 1988, a member of a chaebol family, Chung Mong-joon, president of Hyundai Heavy Industries, successfully ran for South Korea's National Assembly. Other chaebol leaders have also been elected to the National Assembly. Until recently, it has been taken as read that what is good for the chaebol, the country's dominant economic institutions, is good for South Korea.

This 'national champion' status of the chaebol had previously been reflected in the leniency shown to chaebol leaders convicted of crimes. In January 2013, Chey Tae-won, chairman of the third largest chaebol, SK Group, was convicted of embezzlement to cover trading losses and was sentenced to four years in prison. In August 2015, he and other convicted business bosses were pardoned by South Korea's then president, Park Geun-hye, 'to give them a chance', the Ministry of Justice had later explained, 'to develop the country's economy' (3.12).

Opinion polls have revealed that well over half of the country's population are not persuaded by this argument and disapprove of the pardoning of convicted chaebol bosses. This lesson appears to have been learned. A more recent scandal, which has already cost Park Geun-hye her presidency, is centred on Ms Park's relationship with her friend and adviser, Choi Soon-sil. It has featured allegations of influence-peddling and leaks of classified information. One of the scandal's subplots involves Samsung, the largest chaebol, with annual sales equivalent to a fifth of South Korea's GDP.

In August 2017, Samsung Group's de facto head, Lee Jae-yong, was convicted over payments of $36 million to Choi foundations and for giving a horse and several million dollars to help the equestrian career of Choi's daughter. This was in return, prosecutors alleged, for government support for a Samsung restructuring. Lee was jailed for five years for bribery and embezzlement.

He appealed against his conviction. On 5 February 2018, the appeals court halved his sentence and suspended it for four years, allowing Lee to walk free five months after his conviction. He was not pardoned by President Moon Jae-in, but his release was seen as a setback by the reformers. Samsung had announced a stock split in

January, aimed at creating shareholder value and, as if to appease reformers for Lee's controversial release, promised to press ahead with governance reforms.

At the annual general meeting of 23 March, Kim Sun-uk became only the second female director of Samsung in its 49-year history. Samsung also announced the separation of the roles of chairman and CEO and increased the number of board members from nine to eleven.

A year earlier, Samsung had rejected our demands, backed up by Paul Singer's activist vehicle, Elliott Management, to switch to a holding company structure, but did announce plans to accede to our demand to cancel $35 billion of 'treasury' shares with privileged voting rights that had strengthened family control.

Elliott had been a thorn in Samsung's side for some years. In 2015, it objected strongly, but unsuccessfully, to a controversial merger of Samsung affiliates, which it said unfairly benefited the company's founding family at the expense of minority shareholders.

Having exposed the archaic governance arrangements of Samsung, in particular, and of the chaebol model in general, to the glare of international publicity, Elliott turned its attention to Hyundai.

The old-fashioned, some will say medieval, quality of some of the chaebol extends beyond the nepotism evident in appointments to leadership roles and cosy relationships with government. In common with other chaebol, Samsung was also coming under attack for its treatment of employees. In early April 2018, Seoul prosecutors said they were probing allegations that the company had been sabotaging efforts to set up labour unions in South Korea. Unions are anathema to chaebol.

In his foreword to *unFAIR PLAY!*, published by the IndustriAll Global Union (IAGU) in 2014, IAGU's General Secretary Jyrki Raina said that Hyundai was 'a relic from the time of dictatorship' that ran South Korea until 1987. The founding family continues to hold all the important jobs and 'the management structure is autocratic and authoritarian'. Raina added, 'representation of the interests of the workforce is rejected, as is constructive cooperation with trade unions ... this leaves employees exposed to the whims of their managers, usually without any form of protection. The result is that labour relations at Hyundai are more confrontational than at any other car manufacturer' (3.13).

unFAIR PLAY! – the title of the IAGU excoriation of Hyundai's labour relations policies – refers to the group's sponsorship of the 2022 football FIFA World Cup and calls on the group to begin negotiations on an 'international framework agreement' for industrial relations at its Hyundai Motor Company and Kia Motors subsidiaries.

Industrial relations policies of this kind contravene various international conventions such as the UN's Universal Declaration of Human Rights and International Covenant on Economic, Social and Cultural Rights and also the OECD Guidelines for Multinational Enterprises. They worry investors because they increase the risks of damaging industrial disputes and consumer boycotts.

Hyundai, owner of the Hyundai and Kia brands, has been hit by persistent labour unrest in recent years. For a sixth consecutive year, workers held strikes that disrupted the carmaker's production for thirteen days in 2017. They downed tools again for several hours in December 2018, in protest against the company's refusal to accept their demands for a 7.2 per cent rise in the basic wage and a bonus that amounts to a third of the company's net profits.

Other problems for Hyundai include poor sales because of the company's lack of a sports utility vehicle (SUV) and pressure from antitrust regulators to simplify the cross-ownership structures among its subsidiaries and associates. Having responded to the latter by announcing a major group-restructuring proposal on 28 March 2018, the controlling Chung family could have been forgiven for feeling besieged when, a few days later, Elliott Management announced that it had purchased a $1 billion stake in the company and its main subsidiaries. Elliott said it would press for governance reforms and more details on how Hyundai would optimise balance sheets and enhance capital returns at each of the group companies.

On 21 May 2018, Hyundai Motor responded by announcing that it was shelving a controversial restructuring within days of a plea to shareholders by its top executives to support it. The $8.8 billion deal would have involved the sale, by Hyundai's controlling Chung family, of its 30 per cent stake in the group's logistics unit, Hyundai Glovis, and the family's purchase of more shares of Hyundai Mobis, the parts unit at the centre of the group's ownership structure. Elliott and other minority shareholders opposed the plans because they would have strengthened the Chung family's control (3.14).

The deal had been due to go to the vote on 29 May, but in the preceding weeks Elliott had been joined by proxy advisors Institutional Shareholder Services (ISS) and Glass Lewis & Co in opposing the plans. 'The board has failed to articulate a clear business rationale for the transaction, and has not provided any details in support of the purported synergies,' ISS said in mid-May.

The plans had to be shelved after the two proxy advisors took a stand against them because they required a two-thirds majority to pass and foreign investors owning 49 per cent of Hyundai Mobis would have blocked it.

The chaebol are encircled. Pressure for reform is coming from their government, from foreign investors demanding simplifications of the complex cross-shareholdings designed to retain control in family hands, and from chaebol employees demanding higher pay and better working conditions. They have served South Korea well as the chief agents of the country's post-war industrialisation. But the support they have had from government, ranging from guaranteed loans in the early years to more recent presidential pardons for convicted executives, seems inappropriate in this day and age. And family control, maintained at the expense of minority shareholders, is an anachronism.

Public opinion has also been outraged by the arrogance displayed by members of chaebol dynasties. In 2014, Heather Cho, the 44-year-old heiress of Hanjin Group, which controls Korean Air and its hotel chain, was so incensed by the way cabin crew served macadamia nuts on an international Korean Air flight from New York, that she ordered the pilot to taxi back to the gate so that the cabin crew chief could be removed from the flight. In 2015, an appeals court found Ms Cho guilty of using violence against flight attendants and sentenced her to ten months in prison, suspended for two years.

Investors also worry about the risks the chaebol can pose for investment in start-ups and small and medium-sized enterprises in South Korea. The founder of a successful bakery business that we had invested in told us how he had come face to face with chaebol power in a Seoul nightclub. When he complained about the noise a group of chaebol executives were making, he was summoned to their table. 'How would you like me to go into the bakery business?' the chaebol family member asked him.

Institutions that deliberately or inadvertently suppress the nation's entrepreneurial spirit have outlived their usefulness. Because it violates the principles of modern corporate governance, the chaebol's organisational model is likely to become one of the most prominent scalps of active investors in emerging markets. The underlying businesses will not be dismantled altogether, but they will be obliged to adapt. At this stage, it seems likely that they will initially develop into Western-style conglomerates and could then be broken up into their constituent parts through IPOs. A number of large subsidiaries already have separate listings, so it would not be a huge step to reduce family holdings to below the level of effective control.

Reaching decisions

According to the philosopher Karl Popper (1902–94), the central question in democracy is not, 'Who should rule?' but, 'How can we so organise political institutions that bad, or incompetent rulers can be prevented from doing too much damage?' (3.15).

This distinction between the position of ruler and the system of ruling, or 'governance', is as important for investors as it is for democrats. In both cases, the system of governance offers some protection to constituents from the risk that their interests will be compromised by dishonest, incompetent or self-serving leaders.

We do not agree with the English historian and moralist, Lord Acton, that 'Great men are almost always bad men,' but we recognise the danger he identified that: 'Power tends to corrupt and absolute power corrupts absolutely.' We also recognise that corruption risk, illustrated by such emerging market scandals as Petrobras, Asia Pulp and Paper, Cukurova and Steinhoff, is not confined to countries with low CPI rankings. Names such as Enron, Parmalat, Elf, Madoff, WorldCom, Volkswagen and Kobe Steel attest to the pervasiveness of the misuse and abuse of power in business, in mature as well as emerging markets.

Perceptions of corruption contribute to a country's so-called 'risk premium', the additional return investors require to offset perceived risks of investing in that country, including political instability, exchange rate risks, and economic uncertainties such as national indebtedness and Brexit.

When choosing between countries, economic growth rates are of the first importance to investors, but background conditions such as the CPI ranking and the overall Country Risk Premium will help to determine how much of the value created by that economic growth is likely to feed through to shareholders in local companies.

By the same token, when choosing companies in the country to invest in, the quality of the company's governance code and the rigour with which it is applied and complied with in practice will help determine how much of the value the company creates is likely to feed through to minority shareholders.

Background conditions

Corruption Perceptions Index scores and Country Risk Premiums are useful measures of investment risk. For passive funds that invest or divest according to changes in the composition of indices, they may be sufficient to determine geographical asset allocation.

But they are broad-brush measures. They lack the resolution to drill down and find diamonds in the rough: companies that could be good investments despite their countries' low CPIs and high CRPs.

Active investors have a higher-resolution lens, and will look for companies in countries that the passive funds ignore, that display the potential for, rather than the fact of, ESG compliance.

The impression one has of the attractiveness of a country for investors is affected by the level at which one engages with it. A country that seems to be incompetent and corrupt at the political or administrative level at the same time might appear dynamic and innovative at the level of its businesses. If you steer clear of all badly run countries you are going to miss a large number of profitable, well-run companies.

We are the first to acknowledge, however, that the attractions to investors of companies of all sizes in emerging markets depend, to a significant extent, on general background conditions. We mean by this, not simply that Corruption Perceptions Index rankings and Country Risk Premiums vary, but also that institutional frameworks and prevailing macroeconomic conditions and attitudes to business differ, too.

We apply what we call the FELT test to potential investments:

Is it Fair – Are all investors treated equally?
Is it Efficient – Can the stock be bought and sold easily and safely?

Is the market in the shares Liquid – Are there enough in issue and is volume high enough to ensure accurate pricing?

Is it Transparent – Is relevant information readily available?

The first and fourth are to do with corporate governance. The second and third are more to do with institutional frameworks, for example: the availability or lack of banking and custody services; the existence or lack of regulated local markets for capital and commodities; the stability, consistency and business-friendliness of statute and case law; and the independence of the judiciary.

A high priority for any government wishing to attract foreign investment is to ensure the environment for business and finance within its borders is sufficiently favourable to persuade at least one of the major players in the global custody market to establish a presence there. We will not invest in Iran, for example, because none of the big global custody players cover the country.

National institutional frameworks vary, but, to be attractive to investors, they must include a set of reasonable and generally accepted rules. In his book, *Europe Incorporated*, Gianni Montezemolo suggested there was a difference between attitudes to rules in Northern and Southern European countries (3.16). He said that, generally speaking, Northern Europeans do not like rules but tend to abide by the few they have, whereas Southern Europeans love making rules but, in practice, do not tend to take much notice of them.

When we talk of the need for 'rules-based governance' of both countries and companies, we mean governance systems based on rules that are accepted as necessary for good governance, are not subject to summary changes and are generally respected. Rules are useless if they do not regulate behaviour and if no sanctions are imposed on those who break them. An investor in emerging markets has plenty of uncertainty and risk to worry about, without having to wonder if the rules on which his or her investment decisions may have been partly based will be changed without notice or routinely flouted, with impunity, by competitors and supply chain neighbours.

An important set of rules for investors are those relating to rights and the protection of those rights, for example: property rights; the rights of minority shareholders; the right to a fair trial; rights ensuring the independence of the judiciary and equality before the law; and the right of appeal against the decisions of regulators, officials and administrators.

We will discuss governance reform in emerging markets in more detail in the next chapter but, before that, we want to make one final point about corporate governance here. As the prime mover of ESG investment, it is not simply a measure of the attractions of a company for investors. For active investors, it is also the lever or instrument with which they can help transform ugly ducklings into swans.

4

Reforming G

When we arrived at Lagos International Airport, we were greeted by a sign that read: 'Welcome to Lagos, the centre of excellence'. A little way beyond the sign, there were 20 old-fashioned immigration desks wrapped in plastic that appeared never to have been used.

Moving on through the crowded and sweltering terminal, we were confronted by a tough-looking immigration and customs official, who thoroughly scanned our passports and then our luggage.

'What is the purpose of your visit to Nigeria?' he asked.

'Business.'

'What kind of business?'

'Investment.'

'What kind of investment?'

'Investments in companies.'

'Which companies?'

On the wall behind the official, Mark saw a hoarding that was advertising a local milk products brand. We had nothing to do with the company, but Mark offered its name in reply to the official's question. The official seemed satisfied and passed us through.

In the car taking us to the hotel, Mark was scanning his phone for news. Mo Ibrahim – the Sudanese-British billionaire founder of the Mo Ibrahim Foundation – had launched the annual Ibrahim Prize for Achievement in African Leadership.

After checking in at the hotel and unpacking in our rooms, we found the water from the bathroom taps was brown. On his way back down to the lobby, Carlos got stuck in the elevator. He shouted for help, but eventually had to climb out. The 'centre of excellence' could have used a few upgrades.

But, despite these less than excellent qualities, despite the Western management soundbites, the traffic, the pollution and the poverty, Lagos works. Since the federal government moved to Abuja in 1991 and the administration of the former capital fell into the hands of business people, rather than politicians, Lagos state has taken off. Its population has doubled over the past decade to 20 million, and according to official estimates its output in 2017 was $136 billion, more than a third of Nigeria's GDP and significantly more than the GDP of Kenya. Its nominal per capita income of over $5,000 is more than double the Nigerian average.

Lagos is the centre of Nigeria's manufacturing and 'home to a pan-African banking industry, as well as a thriving music, fashion and film scene ... More recently, it has become a tech hub to rival Nairobi's so-called 'Silicon Savannah' (4.1).

'In the past 18 years, Lagos has transformed,' Lamido Sanusi, a former central bank governor and now Emir of the northern city of Kano, told the *Financial Times* in March 2018. 'In terms of roads, in terms of infrastructure, in terms of governance, in terms of a general investment environment, in terms of security, the [Lagos] government has given people a greater opportunity to thrive.'

Mark and Carlos were visiting the city a few years earlier to check out a bank we were thinking of investing in, and attend the annual shareholders' meeting of a brewery we had already invested in. Our itinerary also included a trip to Abuja to meet Sanusi. He was still central bank governor at the time. Back in Lagos, we felt something of what Sanusi would describe five years later. The city seemed safe and there was a strong undercurrent of energy and vitality. Tourists find the persistence of hucksters, hustlers and street traders irritating. We like it. It is a sign that, whatever people say about the integrity of politicians and public officials in Abuja or the quality of infrastructure, there is a hunger among the people of Lagos, including the growing number of migrants from rural areas, for a better life.

Reform creates value

An attribute of investments in emerging markets that is not shared by investments in mature markets is the possibility that shares will rise across the board as a consequence of improvements in the country's standards of governance. In other words, there is always a chance that a country's risk premium will fall. And all other things being equal, a reduction in the country's risk premium will tend to push the share prices of all its companies higher.

We take a view on such possibilities and assign probabilities to them. We do the same when looking for businesses to invest in. We will not invest in a badly run company unless we think there is a good chance that pressure from us and other shareholders will lead to actual reform rather than mere promises of reform.

As experienced, well-informed, long-term shareholders, we have a certain amount of influence on boards and other investors, that we use to push for governance reforms at companies in which we invest.

We do not have much direct influence on politicians, political parties or factions, although we are consulted by politicians from time to time as representatives of the foreign investors they wish to attract. We make it our business, however, to try to understand the country's political dynamics, and the strength of the pressure for reform, so that we can assess the chance of significant reform within our investment time horizon.

In other words, there are two dimensions of governance reform – a 'macro' dimension at the level of the country, and a 'micro' dimension at the level of the firm. Both are value-creating. Macro reform creates value by improving the environment for business. It can involve several elements: reduced corruption demonstrated by a move up Transparency International's CPI (see p. 63) league table; a strengthening of property rights and the rule of law; better compliance with the national tax code; better-paid and more competent public officials; increased budgets for infrastructure; fairer and firmer regulations; and more stable prices. Micro reforms, at the level of the firm, create value for the firm's shareholders by making the company more attractive to existing and prospective customers, employees and investors. In so doing, it creates jobs, brings more money into the local community and enlarges the economy.

Macro reform

Each emerging market is different. Each follows its own pattern of development and reform. But we have found there is always pressure for reform in countries suffering under corrupt, kleptocratic and incompetent governments. Its nature and extent, and the ease with which it can be expressed, will vary, as will the speed with which the reforms it leads to are introduced. But the pressure is always there, waiting for a door to open: a change of regime, perhaps, or some other discontinuity that disrupts the corrupt or incompetent governance status quo.

How quickly reforms are implemented will obviously affect the timing of the market's re-rating, and, in general, investors would be wise to be patient after a reform programme has been announced. Sometimes, however, when the hunger for reform among ordinary people is strong, it can happen surprisingly quickly.

Mikheil Saakashvili, leader of the bloodless 'Rose Revolution' in Georgia in late 2003, replaced Eduard Shevardnadze as president in January 2004, a month after his thirty-seventh birthday. At the time, Georgia was a deeply troubled country, notable for widespread poverty, high crime rates, crumbling infrastructure (frequent power cuts and dilapidated schools and hospitals), and rampant corruption. No one relished the prospect of investing in a country that ranked 133 out of 145 in Transparency International's CPI league table.

Initially, Georgia's problems appeared to be compounded by the new government. Its pro-Western foreign policy and declared intent to join NATO and the European Union compromised its relations with Russia, its largest trading partner. Angered by Georgia's plan to leave Russia's 'sphere of influence', the Kremlin banned imports of Georgian wine in 2006, severed all financial links between the two countries and put up the price at which it sold gas to Georgia.

Two years later, war broke out and Russia annexed two regions in the north of Georgia: Abkhazia and South Ossetia. Both are seen today by the international community as Georgia's territory, under Russian occupation.

We travelled around Georgia after Saakashvili took office and talked to business people. We sensed something was happening: that the roots of the Rose Revolution ran deeper than we had supposed and that something quite different from the Georgia of the recent past was emerging. Whatever it was, perhaps a hunger for a simpler and more honest way of life, it turned out to be much more important than Russia's trade embargo and more expensive gas.

Saakashvili, and his pro-West, pro-NATO government, took this poor, economically anaemic, corrupt, Russian-dominated country by the scruff of its neck, and shook it vigorously in the belief that there was another, healthier Georgia trying to get out. They fired all civil servants, including police officers, only rehired those not implicated in or suspected of corruption, and raised their pay to the point where they could make a decent living, without taking bribes. Many of the oligarchs who had previously dominated Georgia's economy were arrested. Most agreed to pay large fines in exchange for their release. The new government cut red tape, simplified the tax system, cracked down on tax evasion and launched an ambitious privatisation programme. Higher tax yields, plus proceeds from the privatisations, quadrupled government revenues in three years and provided the capacity for substantial public spending on services and infrastructure.

Water and power utilities were made to operate reliably, schools and hospitals were renovated, and the government invested heavily in new roads and housing.

Despite the deterioration in relationships with Russia, these reforms and policies had a dramatic and surprisingly swift impact on the country's fortunes. The economic growth rate accelerated and reached 12 per cent in 2007, just before the financial crash, making Georgia one of the fastest-growing economies in Eastern Europe. The World Bank dubbed Georgia 'the number one economic reformer in the world' on the strength of an improvement from 112 to 18 in the three years to 2008, in the World Bank's Ease of Doing Business (EDB) ranking.

In 2011, Georgia's parliament passed the Economic Liberty Act, restricting the government's ability to intervene in the economy, and setting reduction targets for public spending and borrowing of 30 and 60 per cent, respectively. This Act also stipulated that tax rates and structures could not be changed without a popular referendum.

Perhaps most significant for investors, Georgia's CPI ranking soared from 133 (out of 145) in 2004, well below Russia, to 67 (out of 180) in 2008, 80 places above Russia. By the time Saakashvili left office in 2013 after his maximum two presidential terms, it ranked 51 out of 175. This extraordinary transformation in the prevailing national ethos could not have happened in the absence of a strong popular hunger for such a change.

For us, one of the most impressive features of these Georgian reforms was the Saakashvili administration's understanding of the importance of symbolism, exemplified by the Public Service Hall in the capital, Tbilisi. Designed by Italian architect, Massimiliano Fuksas, the ultra-modern building consists of a roof of tall white mushrooms, with slender stems, covering a glass office block. It is a one-stop shop for the public's interactions with civil servants, such as obtaining licences, passports, trade registrations, etc. Its transparency symbolises the government's new ethos of openness and honesty. Its beauty implies that such qualities are modern and 'cool', and that corruption and bribery are outdated and uncool.

After the defeat of Saakashvili's United National Movement in the 2012 parliamentary election, he was succeeded as president in November 2013 by Giorgi Margvelashvili. By then, much of the power of the presidential office had been transferred, by changes to the constitution, to the office of prime minister, occupied by Bidzina Ivanishvili, billionaire leader of the Georgian Dream coalition.

Soon after he took office, Prime Minister Ivanishvili invited us to Tbilisi to discuss foreign investment in Georgia. Before the meeting, we were given a guided tour of the Public Service Hall. We were impressed, not only by the transparency of the building, but also by the openness, efficiency and transparency of a government office, in a country that was previously notorious for its corrupt officials. We were told during our tour that the catalyst for this seemingly miraculous transformation was the former president's firing of virtually all civil servants and their subsequent rehiring, based on qualifications alone.

We also found the tour reassuring because it suggested that Ivanishvili was proud of the building and what it symbolised, and that, despite the fact that his coalition included radical nationalists and pro-Russian former members of the Shevardnadze administration, the new government was unlikely to repudiate Saakashvili's reforms and pro-Western orientation. So it proved. By 2017, Georgia's CPI ranking was up to 46.

At a subsequent meeting with Ivanishvili, at his home, he asked our advice on how to improve Georgia's reputation as an attractive investment destination. Discussions revolved around establishing a government fund to co-invest with private funds in local firms. We emphasised the importance of a strong legal framework to protect private businesses and a rule-based economy. No one understood the importance of these things better than Ivanishvili, who had himself built a large and successful business. The main difference between his and Saakashvili's outlook was that he favoured a more cordial relationship with Russia, Georgia's largest trading partner.

After this meeting, we called at the offices of a large local bank, in which we had a 10 per cent equity stake. The investment had been made after our tour in the early days of Saakashvili's first term as president. We were putting the puzzle together, looking at the structural changes at the political and macroeconomic levels, and focusing on what they meant for institutions. This particular bank attracted our attention because it had hired a Georgian from the International Finance Corporation (IFC) as its CEO. The IFC is a member of the World Bank Group and offers investment, advisory and fund-management services to encourage private-sector investment in developing countries.

The new CEO followed the government's example: he fired some of the older employees, hired experienced bankers and turned the bank into a professional institution. He came to us, as potential shareholders, and said: 'If you want to become an investor, would you want someone on the board to represent you and the other shareholders?' We bought our 10 per cent after we became comfortable about oversight, governance and the people involved. We interviewed the senior executives and line managers, talked to other shareholders, including the IFC, and sent 'mystery shoppers' into a few branches to see how the changes in the rules were working.

The bank is a big success story. It is run by young, ambitious managers, many of whom had previously worked for a multinational institution. They wanted to set an example for best practice, good corporate governance, highly transparent, proper representation of minority owners on the board and a commitment to keeping all their shareholders well informed. These guys were in the vanguard of a new Georgian ethos that preferred to win, without cheating; to win while playing by the rules.

The same thing is happening in Africa, although not at the same speed. The wealth, the knowledge, the human capital is there; you just have to unlock it by putting it into a proper framework. The brother of the CEO of the Georgian bank we had invested in started a consulting firm to advise countries on how to reform themselves. He has worked for a number of African governments, including those of Ghana and Rwanda. He has found the central one-stop shop for interaction with the government, instead of leaving it to villages and mayors, to be very effective.

An echo of another feature of Saakashvili's muscular approach to reform was the detention in the Ritz-Carlton Hotel in Riyadh of Saudi princes, senior government officials and businessmen, during Crown Prince Mohammed bin Salman's anti-corruption campaign, begun in 2017. The prices for the freedom of these Saudi Arabian equivalents of Georgia's oligarchs were reported to have been payment of large fines.

Micro reform

Governance reform at the level of the firm occurs in response to a variety of pressures, both internal and external. To attract and keep good people, firms need to minimise cronyism and nepotism in senior management appointments and, to attract capital, firms in emerging markets need to comply with the ESG requirements of their foreign investors.

There are some recurring themes in our efforts to bring about governance reform at the level of the firm. We see the composition of boards as important evidence of the seriousness with which companies take their responsibilities to minority shareholders. We see dividend policies, the frequency and transparency of reporting and the degree to which the interests of executives are linked, through their remuneration packages, to the company's performance and share price, as being of fundamental interest to outside investors.

We are not Adam Smith's eighteenth-century investors, who 'seldom pretend to understand anything of the business of the company ... [and] receive contentedly such half-yearly, or yearly dividends as the directors think proper to make them' (see p. 117). We hope to be well informed and opinionated. If our demands for more representative boards, fair distribution policies and the alignment of executive and shareholder interests are not being heeded, we will sell our shares.

Macro via micro

It is simplistic to suggest that the macro is merely the sum of the micros, but there is no denying that, when it comes to governance reform, the macro and micro are intimately connected. Macro reform both enables and is enabled by micro reform. In an economic sense, reform at the level of the firm is what reform at the level of the country is for.

Macro reformers understand this. For example, Prime Minister Ivanishvili invited us to talk with him on two occasions because he wanted to understand what Georgia had to do in order to attract more foreign investment. As already reported (see p. 101), we emphasised the importance of a strong, legal framework and a rules-based economy. We made a similar impression on another government in Eastern Europe, but in a very different way.

In the middle of December 2008, as business was winding down in the run-up to Christmas, a public announcement appeared. Tenders were invited for the mandate to manage Fondul Proprietatea (Fondul), a large investment fund set up by the Romanian government in 2005. If we were interested, we had to submit a tender by the end of the year.

Before deciding whether it was worth working through Christmas and New Year's Eve to meet the deadline, we needed to answer two questions: is it an attractive mandate and what are our chances of winning?

The second was relatively easy to answer – we did not think we stood a snowball's chance in hell of winning. We found out later that we were among 25 bidders, in what is known in the trade as the 'beauty contest' for the mandate: half local, half foreign. Among the latter were such heavyweights as Morgan Stanley and BlackRock. We thought it highly likely that there would be a preference for a local firm, and even if that hurdle could be overcome, the foreign beneficiary was sure to be one of the big names. We thought we had more experience in emerging and frontier markets than most of the other beauty contestants, but we could not imagine a plausible set of circumstances from which we would emerge with the mandate.

And yet ...

We decided to go for it and ruin our Christmases, because the answer to that first question was, 'Yes.' We did find the idea of managing Fondul attractive. It was a large, €4 billion, closed-end fund. We felt we were well equipped to run it: we knew the country well, and we were familiar with the types of companies in its portfolio. We expected to have a free management hand because the Romanian government, Fondul's owner, had declared its intention to list the shares on stock markets in the near future and further reduce its ownership. The origins and aims of the fund were also intriguing.

After the end of the Second World War, at the start of the hegemony of the Soviet Union in Eastern Europe, the commanding heights of the Romanian economy were nationalised without compensation. After the bloody Romanian Revolution of December 1989, the conviction of President Nicolae Ceauşescu for economic sabotage and genocide, and his immediate execution on Christmas Day, claims for compensation by people whose assets had been nationalised four decades earlier were lodged with the courts. The lawsuits dragged on for a decade and a half, until a new Romanian government boldly announced that everyone, including foreigners, as well as Romanian citizens, with valid claims would be compensated for any assets confiscated under communism, at today's value. This was unusual. In most former Soviet Union countries, potential compensation for confiscated assets was considerably below current market values.

This pledge of full compensation was to be effected in one of two ways. If the assets concerned still existed, and were clearly identifiable as the same assets as those that had been confiscated after the war, they were simply handed back. Bran Castle, commonly known as Dracula's Castle, was one such. In 2006, its ownership was transferred from the state to Dominic von Habsburg, the American son of its pre-war owner, Princess Ileana of the Romanian royal family. Assets that could not be identified in this way, because, for example, they had long since been dismembered and the various parts transferred to other entities, were approved and valued by a government agency. In lieu of their original assets, the successful claimants were given shares in Fondul Proprietatea, which had been formed for the purpose in 2005, with a nominal value equivalent to the value of the agreed claim.

Nominal values are one thing, of course, and market values are quite another. Before Fondul's listing, there was no market value but there was substance to the shares, in the form of substantial minority stakes (usually about 20 per cent) in Romanian utilities and some other companies that had always been state-owned.

Fondul began life wholly owned by the Romanian government and managed by government officials. It was announced, at the time of its formation, that independent managers would be appointed within a year and the shares would be publicly listed.

It was an elegant solution to the compensation challenge and amounted, or would amount, once Fondul was listed, to the partial privatisation of the state-owned enterprises in which Fondul held shares. But the government's commitments to an early appointment of outside managers and a subsequent listing were not fulfilled.

This was partly because of the enormous volume of claims that the government was handling: around 70,000 in all. Only about 15,000 had been processed by the time the Fondul management mandate was put out to tender in December 2008. The delay was in the interests of wheeler-dealers hovering around the compensation system in general, and around Fondul in particular, looking for a quick buck.

These wheeler-dealers employed two devices for extracting value. First, they approached compensation claimants and offered to buy their claims before they had been approved, for a fraction of what they were likely to be worth once approved. They would then push the claim through the approval process, which, once completed, would increase the claim's value in Fondul shares by a multiple of three or four. The claims were submitted to, reviewed and valued by ANRP, a state agency created for this purpose. (A number of its officials were later investigated, charged and convicted.)

Second, they started trading Fondul shares between each other on a so-called 'grey' market, operating through a nondescript booth next to Bucharest's main train station. Grey market prices at this stage varied between 10 and 30 per cent of the nominal value of the shares.

Most of the potential from such stratagems had been extracted by 2008, and the wheeler-dealers were ready for the big pay-off on public listing, when the Fondul shares were expected to trade at a price substantially higher than the grey market price. By then, Fondul's largest private shareholders were a couple of Jewish-American families, whose antecedents had been the leading industrialists in Romania before the war.

Interesting history. Interesting fund. We knew our chances of winning were slim but we tendered for it. Much to our surprise, we survived the first round, along with five others: Morgan Stanley, ING, Aviva, Unicredit and BlackRock. Much to ours and to the other short-listed bidders' surprise, no local firms had made it through to the second round. There were two names on the final shortlist, ours and Morgan Stanley, and we emerged as the winner. But you learn not to count chickens too early in Romania.

Representations were made to the special Selection Commission which had run the tender process, objecting to and supporting our appointment. We found out subsequently that the US ambassador to Romania, Mark Gitenstein, was among those who were keeping a close eye on the situation. He cared deeply about Romania and the need for transparency and the rule of law, as well as Fondul's American shareholders. The issue of the Fondul mandate may have been caught up in wider diplomatic conversations between the USA and Romania. The countries are close allies. Both are members of NATO and, much to the disgust of Russia's President Vladimir Putin, Romania hosts the USA's Aegis medium-range missile system.

The Selection Commission eventually confirmed us as winner of the tender process to manage Fondul. But we were not there yet. We also had to get the official approval of Fondul's shareholders and this proved far from a formality. At a shareholders' meeting called to approve our appointment in July 2009, the government, which was still the holder of a majority of Fondul's shares, was conspicuous by its absence. We never found out why. After the meeting, Daniela Lulache, the state-appointed CEO of Fondul's administration at the time, suggested: 'Maybe you haven't done everything you should have done.' We were frustrated and ready to throw in the towel. Private Fondul shareholders and the US ambassador urged us to be patient. 'Don't give up,' Gitenstein said. 'There's a lot at stake here.' After his appointment to Bucharest had ended, the former ambassador accepted an invitation from shareholders to join the Fondul board as an independent director.

So we waited. And eventually our patience was rewarded with a change of government. The new administration agreed to honour the results of the tender process and to give us the mandate. We were officially appointed at a shareholders' meeting on 29 September 2010. Four months later, Fondul's shares were listed on the Stock Exchange. The ordinary shares, with a nominal value of 1 leu, had been changing hands on the grey market at 20–25 cents. Early trading on the public market was at 65 cents.

In September 2010, we began putting Fondul representatives on the boards of the SoEs, of which Fondul and the state were the only shareholders. We also wanted to create a level playing field for all Fondul shareholders. Voting rights for private Fondul shareholders had been capped. We demanded the removal of all such voting restrictions in order to ensure one share, one vote, regardless of ownership. This was not to everyone's liking. Some shareholders with vested interests in the status quo called for a general shareholder meeting (GSM) at a day's notice, at which they planned, we assumed, to instruct us to desist from pressing for SoE board representation and the removal of preferred rights. The backlash fizzled out when we, and other shareholders, pointed out that the planned meeting would be unlawful because Romanian company law required 30 days' notice for a general meeting. This 30-day notice period was routinely flouted by the state, represented by the government's representatives. They were in the habit of calling for GSMs overnight, without proper documentation. We challenged the practice in the courts and were successful.

In the meantime, we had been going through the books of our SoE portfolio companies, looking for signs of corruption. We discovered it was widespread. Hidroelectrica was a case in point. Our 20 per cent of the company was Fondul's second-largest investment, accounting for 20 per cent of the fund. It had to perform if Fondul was to discharge its duty to its shareholders.

The company is the largest pure hydroelectric power company in Europe, with six gigawatts of generating capacity. But until 2010, it had been reporting minimal operating profits or small losses. This seemed odd, because most of the costs in hydropower are from the interest on debt taken out to build hydropower facilities such as dams and turbines, and this debt was not significant. The operating margins should be good because there are no fuel costs.

Our investigations pointed to power-trading arrangements, and we asked for documents relating to them. When the company appeared reluctant to supply them, we said that as an SoE, Hidroelectrica had clear reporting responsibilities that should be enforced. We said that we would have to take legal action against the management and the board if they did not comply with our requests.

The documents duly arrived. They showed that a small group of private electricity traders had long-term contracts to buy power from Hidroelectrica at fixed prices that were sometimes at barely half the market price. We asked the managers to explain. The CEO said the banks wanted the security of long-term contracts. We asked him to terminate the contracts because they were clearly against the interests of shareholders. We estimated that these private traders were making €300 million a year, simply by re-invoicing. Fondul owned 20 per cent of the company. That meant its shareholders were losing out to the tune of €60 million a year.

The terms of the contracts were grotesquely unbalanced in the private traders' favour. Not only were they paying a ridiculously low price for electricity, they could also terminate the contracts whenever they wanted, at no cost, whereas Hidroelectrica could not terminate without heavy penalties. But the contracts were legal so nothing could be done, according to the company.

We were not content to leave it at that, and we published the contracts on our website. All hell broke loose. The story remained headline news in the press for several months. It was the biggest corruption scandal ever in Romania.

The furore over the contracts had politicised the affair and the government was keen to defuse the situation. Its solution was to declare the company insolvent because of the huge contingent liabilities represented by the contracts with the so-called 'smart guys'. The insolvency would render the contracts null and void and pre-empt breach-of-contract claims by the traders. Unsurprisingly, the traders objected. The court ruled that, because Hidroelectrica was insolvent, the administrator appointed by the creditors had the legal right to cancel the contracts.

The judicial administrator, Remus Borza, was great. We worked with him on restructuring the company, cancelling the contracts and preparing for the inevitable appeals by the traders. After yet another change of government, efforts were made to replace Borza, but they could not fire him because he represented the creditors. On his watch, Hidroelectrica enjoyed a huge turnaround and began to make real money. At the time of writing (early 2018), it was making profits at the rate of €300 million a year.

Having forced the cancellation of one type of disadvantageous contract, we were keen to prevent the emergence of others. We were fortunate that the International Monetary Fund (IMF) was active in Romania at that time, in connection with its bailout loan, one helpful condition of which was a Corporate Governance Law for SoEs, obliging them to have independent directors to ensure independent management. We worked with the IMF to strengthen the electricity exchange (OPCOM) in Romania and to oblige generators to sell through OPCOM and only through OPCOM.

Looking back at his period in Bucharest as Fondul's portfolio manager, Greg sees it as testament to the power of good governance rules for companies to trigger reform and the hunger for reform in the whole country. 'We hired five Romanian analysts,' he recalls. 'Initially, they were reluctant to rock the boat, by challenging the status quo. I told them we had to set the rules, but they thought I was being too aggressive. By the end, they had got a taste for it, and I was having to rein them in.'

By September 2017, Fondul's net asset value was $2.72 billion, making it one of the world's largest listed funds. Its portfolio included minority stakes in a score of SoEs, including Hidroelectrica, which was earmarked for an initial public offering (IPO). The Romanian economy was performing strongly and recorded an 8.8 per cent year-on-year growth rate in the third quarter of 2017. It was still benefiting from the reforms in 2009, when public sector wages and pensions were cut as a condition of an International Monetary Fund (IMF) bailout.

By 2016, Romania had climbed into the top third of Transparency International's CPI. But the operating environment for Fondul began to change for the worse after the Social Democratic government came to power in December 2016. It began to revive old practices that threatened to undermine the progress made in recent years in reducing corruption and improving governance.

As Fondul's portfolio manager, Greg was concerned. He said the government had been replacing independent SoE directors with loyal cronies, and was fearful of the consequences of Parliament's plans to introduce legislation that would exempt SoEs from the corporate governance rules.

Greg argued that the implications of such moves for investors went way beyond the companies directly concerned. 'A lot of state companies are either in energy or infrastructure,' he said at the time. 'If you, as a foreign direct investor, see that there's not going to be an improvement in infrastructure such as roads, or see that bad management may mean ports or airports are not going to be able to cut their fees, you won't invest in those sectors.'

He warned that such developments could make the investment climate less attractive, require the deferral of long-awaited IPOs and delay the plans of index company MSCI (formerly Morgan Stanley Capital International) to promote Romania from a 'frontier' to an 'emerging' market. This was very important for Romania because it would open up the country to a broader range of investors.

Energy Minister Toma Petcu insisted that Hidroelectrica's IPO was still on track for early 2018 but said only 10 per cent of the equity, rather than the 15 per cent originally planned, would be listed. That might not provide sufficient liquidity to warrant the MSCI upgrade from frontier status. Unhappy with the revisions to the Hidroelectrica listing plans, Fondul was considering selling its 20 per cent stake, which accounted for one-third of its net asset value.

Since then, there has been a change of government and repeated clashes between Fondul and the new administration over governance at SoEs in which they are both shareholders. At a press conference in Bucharest on 14 February 2018, Greg said that before the IPO could take place, Hidroelectrica had to be ready for listing. 'It's not,' he said, 'and there is really no intention, no action from the government to move Hidroelectrica closer to the listing.' He saw no chance of a listing in 2018 and said prospects for a listing in 2019 depended on the government.

This is where the macro and the micro meet. In its efforts to create value for its beneficiaries through 'micro' interventions that have helped to double the profitability of Romania's large SoEs since 2012, Fondul was putting pressure on the government to continue to respect the 'macro' reforms of the IMF bailout. It did so by forcing the government to confront the possibility that the proceeds from the Hidroelectrica IPO would be considerably lower if they persisted with their declared plans to rescind the governance reforms.

Sustainable reform

While Mark was visiting the Lagos bank we were interested in (see p. 95), Carlos had arrived early at the shareholders' meeting of Nigeria's second-largest brewery. He was reviewing his notes and planning to ask the kind of governance questions we usually ask at such meetings. He waved at a few acquaintances, representing other foreign investors. He knew most of them shared his concerns.

After the formal preliminaries had been completed, the meeting was thrown open for questions from the floor. 'Show time,' Carlos muttered to himself. He glanced at his notes and prepared to stand and say his piece. But, in fact, he and the other foreign investors remained seated throughout the rest of the proceedings.

'A couple of local pension fund managers stood up and started asking the questions I was planning to ask,' Carlos recalls:

> I was amazed. I couldn't believe how aggressive, smart and well-informed they were. I had expected the international guys to take the lead, but they didn't say a word. Local pension funds were getting quite large in Nigeria. These two guys had $20 billion or so under management at the time. They took the board to task on dividend payouts, and demanded more transparency on management pay. I will never forget it. The foreign investors were looking at each other, open-mouthed and grinning. 'Wow,' we thought. 'We can relax.'

It was an important moment for us. It meant not only that the local pension funds in Nigeria had become potential allies in our efforts to put pressure on companies to improve their standards of corporate governance, but also that the checks and balances we take for granted were taking root and that in Nigeria, at any rate, responsible, long-term, active local shareholders were emerging.

That's exactly what we want, and what Africa needs.

5

Activism

Investors have never had as much power as they have today. They are not always minded to use it, but, in developed economies, the days when managers of listed companies could afford to ignore importunate investors have passed. This is a new development in the evolution of liberal capitalism, with profound implications for the future allocation of global resources.

After the 'flash crash' we know as the 'South Sea Bubble', the Bubble Act of 1720 in Britain gave joint-stock company investors the gift of limited liability. Since then, they have tended to hold their peace and give their agents (management) a more or less free rein. In 1776, half a century after that crash, Adam Smith noted that investors in joint stock companies: 'seldom pretend to understand anything of the business of the company . . . [and] receive contentedly such half-yearly or yearly dividends as the directors think proper to make them' (5.1).

Things were no different two centuries later, when Adolf Berle (best known for his pre-war collaboration with Gardiner Means on the separation of ownership and control) noted that: 'stockholders, though still politely called "owners", are passive. They have the right to receive only. The condition of their being is that they do not interfere in management' (5.2). In most Western economies today, they have other rights, too: the right to be heard, the right to hire and fire the directors, the right to be kept informed, the right to fair treatment and more.

Investors are supported by an inquisitive press as well as persistent demands from lawmakers and regulators for ever more 'transparency'. This means that, even when in a small minority, they can make their views known in board and executive committee rooms, invoke their rights in statutes and stock exchange listing agreements, appeal to regulators, and alert the financial press when managers and majority shareholders try to ride roughshod over their rights. We say 'can', because a growing number of shareholders choose not to exercise their voting power. Although 'still politely called "owners", [they] are passive'. They 'seldom pretend to understand anything of the business of the company'. They invest, not because of qualities they see in the company, but because the company is a constituent of an index their fund managers have chosen to track. So, although they may profess interest in ESG for marketing reasons, their ESG-branded funds simply track ESG-screened indices. In emerging markets, where coverage of ESG indices is limited, their ESG touch on local companies is so light as to be undetectable. They have power, in theory, but, in practice, nowadays, they prefer to be budget asset managers and not vocal investors.

However, although the trend is towards passive investing, there is at the same time an increase in investor and consumer 'activism', much of which has come to be associated with ESG issues. We will first focus on investor activism and begin by recalling what the active investors of today are being active about.

Fair shares

The residual value created by a company after it has paid its dues to the tax authorities belongs, in theory, to all its shareholders equally, according to the number of shares each owns. In practice, it does not always work out that way. Managers may try to divert a disproportionate amount of the value added into their own pockets, take excessive or unnecessary risks, make unforced errors, pursue suboptimal strategies or concede too much or too little in their negotiations with suppliers, partners, associates or unions. It is part of the board's oversight job to monitor and police these so-called 'agency costs' of management.

Another, more incestuous, form of competition for possession of residual value added that is particularly common in, but by no means confined to, emerging markets, is between shareholders. All shareholders are equal, in theory, but in practice, some, like the pigs in George Orwell's *Animal Farm*, may be more equal than others and may use their actual or effective voting control to rob small shareholders of their fair shares. They may insist, for instance, on dividend payouts, business or marketing strategies, mergers or acquisitions, or management or board appointments that are in their wider interests, rather than in the interests of all of their fellow shareholders.

Devices used to oppress smaller or minority shareholders include complicated cross-shareholdings that give the over-mighty shareholders effective control, with relatively small 'beneficial' ownership. When, for instance, company A holds 51 per cent of company B, which holds 51 per cent of company C, which, in turn, holds 51 per cent of company D, company A effectively controls company D despite the fact that its beneficial ownership is only 13 per cent of D's equity.

Another common way of denying the principle of one share, one vote, at the expense of minority shareholders is for companies to issue non-voting shares, or to retain privileged voting rights for founder shareholders. S&P Dow Jones Indices won plaudits from the investment community in July 2017, when it announced, after the IPO by Snap Inc. (owner of the Snapchat app) of non-voting shares, that companies with more than one class of ordinary share could not join the S&P 500 Index (5.3).

The rights of minority shareholders are embedded in rules and regulations, the stability and even-handedness of which are valued by investors. Therefore, it should have come as no surprise to UK regulators when several institutional shareholders reacted angrily to rule changes designed to attract the postponed IPO of Saudi Aramco to the London market.

The Financial Conduct Authority (FCA) confirmed in June 2018 that it was pressing ahead with the creation of a new category within its 'premium' listing rules that would exempt companies controlled by governments from rules relating to oligarch-owned and private companies. Under the FCA's new rules, a sovereign shareholder would not be treated as 'a related party' and would not, therefore, need shareholder approval for a transaction with the company (5.4). Large institutional investors, including Norges, Norway's oil fund and the world's biggest sovereign wealth fund (see p. 54), objected strongly to these changes, on the grounds that they would weaken the protection of minority investors from decisions by the Saudi government that were against their interests.

Such regulatory bribery notwithstanding, minority shareholders are not powerless when a controlling shareholder tries to deny them their rights, but as noted above, they are not always minded to put their power to the test and claim their rights. In some cases, the passive funds enjoy their rights as shareholders only because they have active co-investors on whose diligence and energy they take a free ride.

Worse than Marxism

According to Thomson Reuters Lipper data, passive funds, including low-cost exchange traded funds (ETFs), manage $8 trillion worth of assets, or about 20 per cent of all investment fund assets worldwide. The figures for equities are even higher. The passive funds manage 30 and 43 per cent of equity assets in Europe and the USA, respectively. These percentages are expected to rise.

Passive funds are increasing their market share because they charge lower fees without imposing substantial extra costs on the investor in the form of serious underperformance. But passive investors abdicate the responsibilities of owners of companies and play no role in shaping economies by allocating resources. They cannot even 'vote with their feet' and sell shares because to do so would compromise their index-tracking accuracy. Some have suggested this withdrawal of owners from engagement with their companies strikes at the heart of capitalism itself.

In August 2016, Inigo Fraser-Jenkins of US brokers Sanford C. Bernstein, published a polemical note entitled, 'The Silent Road to Serfdom: Why Passive Investing is Worse than Marxism'. The title is a reference to Friedrich von Hayek's seminal book, *The Road to Serfdom* (1944), which warned that government control of economic decision-making through central planning would inevitably lead to tyranny. Fraser-Jenkins argued that 'active investment decisions form a crucial part of the capital allocation process . . . a possible alternative is a Marxist economy', in which the allocation of capital is planned. An economy in which investment is passive is even worse, Fraser-Jenkins claims, because it lacks any capital allocation process.

According to this view, passive investors preserve the status quo by allocating all capital to companies already large enough to be constituents of capitalisation-weighted indices. Perhaps because they are conscious of the growing momentum of ESG investing, for which their hitherto hugely successful business model is not well equipped, passive investors seem to believe they have a case to answer here.

In a letter to investors in early 2018, Larry Fink, the CEO of passive fund giant BlackRock, proposed 'a new model of shareholder engagement', which recognised that a 'company's ability to manage environmental, social and governance matters demonstrates the leadership and good governance that is so essential to sustainable growth'. Vanguard, another passive fund giant, has also pledged to 'continue to strengthen our commitment to investment stewardship'.

Proposing a new model of shareholder engagement (new to Larry Fink, anyway), and strengthening a claimed commitment to whatever Vanguard means by 'investment stewardship', is one thing. Becoming a genuinely active investor is quite another.

From raiders to reformers

'Activist' investors have come a long way since the 1980s, when the likes of Carl Icahn and T. Boone Pickens were known, pejoratively, as 'corporate raiders'. There is still some opportunistic raiding going on, but there is an increasing amount of what Claudio Rojas has called 'engaged', as opposed to 'financial', activism, where investors adopt a longer-term approach to extracting value (5.5). As an example of 'engaged' activism, Rojas cites the proxy battles of Bill Ackman's Pershing Square Capital Management, with Canadian Pacific Railway. Other examples of 'engaged' investors include Warren Buffett's Berkshire Hathaway group, Daniel Loeb's Third Point hedge fund and Paul Singer's Elliott Associates.

Shareholder 'activism' employs several stratagems. Writing to and negotiating with management is usually the first step. Daniel Loeb, for example, is known for the asperity of his letters to the CEOs of his target companies. After correspondence come publicity campaigns, litigation and filing resolutions hostile to management at shareholder meetings. The latter may lead to so-called 'proxy battles', when activist investors persuade other investors, some of whom will be passive, to make common cause with them on particular resolutions.

An intriguing proxy battle was played out on 4 April 2018, at a Telecom Italia (TI) board meeting (5.6). In the blue corner was French billionaire Vincent Bolloré's Vivendi group, which held 24 per cent of TI's voting rights. In the red corner was Paul Singer's hedge fund, Elliott Advisors, with 9 per cent of TI's voting rights. Each of the combatants were proposing the election to the board of a different slate of ten directors. In the middle were the 'big three' passive funds – State Street, Vanguard and BlackRock – holding about 7 per cent of TI's shares between them. Press reports ahead of the board meeting suggested the vote would be close, and would hinge on the decision of the passive funds.

At issue was Elliott's contention that Vivendi had treated TI as an extension of Bolloré's business empire and transferred value created by the Italian company upwards to Vivendi rather than to TI's shareholders. Voting rights were a major bone of contention. Groupe Bolloré had effective control of TI despite the fact that it owned only 20 per cent of Vivendi, and the fact that Vivendi owned only 17 per cent of TI's shares (but 24 per cent of TI's voting rights). In other words, Groupe Bolloré's beneficial interest in TI was less than 3.5 per cent.

In the event, Elliott and its allies were victorious, just. Of the 96.6 per cent of the TI equity for which votes were cast, 51.6 per cent backed the directors nominated by Elliott. In a subsequent statement, the hedge fund said that the victory 'sends a powerful signal to Italy and beyond that engaged investors will not accept substandard corporate governance, paving the way to maximising value creation for all TI's shareholders'.

Complicated cross-shareholdings and special shares with extra votes are prime targets for active investors because they allow a founder or outsiders to exercise effective control with relatively little committed capital. They are becoming less common in mature markets because they are seen as bad governance practice, but they remain common in emerging markets. For instance, active investors, including the Elliott group and us, have objected strongly to their routine use in South Korea's chaebol industrial groups (see p. 81). They can also be irksome for investors in the emerging market subsidiaries and associates of multinational companies.

Poland's sour Orange

We were surprised in mid-June 2005 to hear that the 'Idea' brand of the Polish mobile phone operator, Centertel, would be replaced by the Orange brand. We knew the *éminence grise* behind the plan was France Télécom (renamed Orange in 2013), which owned 34 per cent of Centertel and 47.5 per cent of Telekomunikacja Polska (TPSA), owner of the rest of Centertel. We also knew Idea was the most recognised, best regarded and most recommended of Polish mobile brands. As TPSA shareholders we feared the business might suffer when the strong Idea brand was replaced by a brand unknown in Poland. It seemed to us that in its eagerness to forge Orange into a global brand, France Télécom (FT) was putting the Centertel business at risk.

Our surprise became dismay when we found that not only would TPSA pay for the rebranding, but that it would also pay an annual fee of 1.6 per cent of sales for use of the Orange name. We felt this was an abuse of FT's power and against the interests of minority TPSA shareholders.

We knew FT was negotiating with the Polish government to buy another 4 per cent of TPSA's shares, taking its interest to 51.5 per cent. We held 2.5 per cent, so it would be hard to assemble sufficient proxies to force a general meeting. We could 'make some noise', by issuing a press release outlining our objections, but that could hit TPSA's share price. We decided to take the risk, and were rewarded with a piece in *Gazeta Wyborcza* online, under the headline 'Orange Idea Proves Expensive'. It repeated our observation that Deutsche

Telekom was only charging its Hungarian associate 0.2 per cent of revenues for its use of the T-Mobile brand.

We also wrote to TPSA's independent directors, setting out our objections and expressing our surprise at their approval of 'the unfair fee' that FT was forcing on TPSA for use of a brand name of dubious value.

On 19 July, we received a reply from Andrew Seton, the senior independent director. He assured us that the independent directors 'take very seriously their obligation to protect the interests of all shareholders', but said there was no requirement for TPSA's Supervisory Board to vote on a transaction involving a subsidiary (Centertel). He took issue with our suggestion that Orange should pay TPSA for allowing it to use the Orange name in Poland because Orange had 'no traction in Poland'. He claimed Orange was 'one of the most powerful global names in mobile telephony', and predicted that Poles would not find it hard to adopt the brand.

This missed the point. We were not disputing that Orange was a strong brand globally. We were claiming that Idea, the name Orange would replace, was a strong brand in Poland and was creating value for TPSA shareholders.

Seton did not deny the rebranding was useful from FT's point of view, but insisted that it did not, of itself, make it possible 'to dismiss this as a one-sided game'. As we feared, TPSA's minority shareholders were being obliged to finance one belligerent in a global brand war, in the outcome of which they had no interest.

We talked to another discontented shareholder and drafted and sent a joint letter to Jaroslaw Kozlowski, Chairman of the Polish Securities and Exchange Commission, claiming that it was his duty 'to protect minority investors' in such a situation and asking him to conduct a 'formal inquiry into the "Orange" licence fee'.

A few days later, on 4 August, a piece appeared in the Interfax Poland Business News Service. It reported that the SEC had refused to mount an inquiry into the Orange rebranding because Centertel was not a listed company. It quoted local investment analyst Pawel Puchalski: 'The Orange deal clearly lowers the value of TPSA.' He said that if we managed to block the deal or get the licence fee cut, 'that would be very good news indeed from the point of view of minority shareholders'.

On 13 August, we again wrote to Kozlowski, expressing surprise that the Polish SEC did not 'consider parent companies responsible for their wholly controlled subsidiaries'.

This was the crucial point for us. Most regulators, including the SEC in the US, treat listed companies and their subsidiaries as one group. We told Chairman Kozlowski that as foreign investors we were very concerned about the lack of regulatory protection of minority investors in listed companies, controlled by other listed companies. We pointed out that sometimes such 'daughter companies' can be worth more than their parents and their regulatory breaches can destroy value for investors.

Chairman Kozlowski's response was not reassuring. He said the SEC only monitored the compliance of securities issuers with their disclosure obligations on the introduction of new securities. He insisted it was the duty of the supervisory board to supervise a company's activities. If we felt TPSA's board had acted improperly, we should seek legal redress under Polish law.

On 21 September 2005, two days after Centertel's 'Idea' brand had been replaced by Orange, Warsaw Independent Newswire published what amounted to an obituary for the name under the headline, 'Idea Topped Poland's Brand Recognition Rankings'. Quoting from a report by market research firm TNS OBOP, the article said nine out of ten Poles recognized the Idea brand, and this was the 'result of years of marketing efforts and high advertising spending'. Centertel had spent almost $300 million on 120,000 Idea commercials.

Idea's share of Poland's mobile telephony market was some 33 per cent, immediately before the Orange rebranding. At the end of the third quarter of 2017, by which time TPSA had paid Orange about $500 million in licence fees since 2005 for use of the Orange name, Orange's share of the Polish market was 28 per cent. In October 2005, TPSA's market value was $11 billion. By May 2018, it was less than $2 billion.

Looking back over the TPSA affair, we are left with a sour taste in our mouths and the impression of serious governance and regulatory weaknesses. The rebranding and licence arrangement was obviously a material transaction for TPSA's shareholders. It was, therefore, worrying that there was no requirement for TPSA's board to vote on the transaction.

There was also an alarming lack of transparency. TPSA made no attempt to present TPSA's minority shareholders with a rationale for such licence arrangements, which we had calculated, other things being equal, would reduce TPSA profits by about 12 per cent.

The affair also raised questions about the commitment of TPSA management to the creation of value in the form of net profit, for all shareholders. Conspicuous by its absence from the remuneration of senior management was any link to the TPSA share price. We see some sort of share option scheme as an essential guarantor of the alignment of management and investor interests.

It was also worrying that Poland's SEC should see fit to wash its hands of the whole affair on the grounds that Centertel was not listed. TPSA owned 66 per cent of Centertel and consolidated its accounts with its own. The mobile company should, therefore, have been seen as an integral part of TPSA, and, accordingly, the rebranding and licence deal should have been seen by the SEC as potentially unfair to minority investors and thus a suitable case for investigation.

France Télécom, as it was then, should have known better. If it wishes to continue to attract outside investors to help finance its foreign subsidiaries, it must try harder to cultivate a reputation for treating them fairly. TPSA's minority shareholders were not involved in setting the price FT paid for its TPSA shares and should not have been forced, without consultation, courtesy or explanation, to help make the numbers work after the event.

By the same token, if governments want to continue to attract outside investors to help finance their spending, they must honour their commitments to pay interest and make debt repayments by the stipulated due dates.

Argentina's default

When Argentina shocked the world in 2002 by defaulting on its sovereign debt, NML Capital, managed by Elliott Associates, held Argentinian bonds with a nominal value of $630 million.

Most of its fellow bondholders licked their wounds and, with some reluctance, declared a willingness to accept a restructuring of $24 billion of debt, proposed by the Argentine government, worth 30 cents in the dollar. NML and a few other bondholders declined the offer as wholly inadequate and took the Argentine government to court.

It seemed like a David and Goliath battle, with the Argentine government holding all the cards. But Elliott, ringleader of the holdouts, was persistent and relentlessly litigious. It sued the Argentine government for the debt's full value in both the US and UK courts. The UK High Court found against Elliott on the grounds that Argentina had state immunity, but Elliott's appeal to the UK Supreme Court was successful, and the Court ruled that Elliott had the right to seize Argentine property in the UK.

On 2 October 2012, Elliott secured a Ghanaian court order for the arrest of the ARA *Libertad*, a fully rigged-sail training ship owned by Argentina's navy, and berthed, at the time, in a Ghanaian port. Elliott said it would keep the *Libertad*, one of the world's fastest and largest tall ships, until the debts of $1.6 billion awarded by the court were repaid. The Argentine government refused to pay and secured the ship's release when its seizure was judged illegal by the International Tribunal for the Law of the Sea.

In November 2012, a New York court ruled for NML, in what legal experts called the 'sovereign debt trial of the century'. It led to a new restructuring plan by Argentina in March 2013, but this was dismissed, first by a lower court and then by the US Court of Appeals. In another attempt to seize Argentinian assets, NML sued Elon Musk's SpaceX company in March 2014 for two satellite-launch contracts worth $113 million, which were owned by Argentina. The suit was eventually rejected in a California court in 2015, but by then Argentina had lost its appeal to the US Supreme Court and had nowhere else to go.

In February 2016, Argentina's government capitulated and made a new offer to NML and the other holdouts, worth the equivalent of 75 cents in the dollar. The offer was accepted – Activists 1, Argentina 0. A sovereign state had accepted the judgement of the courts and paid the price for regaining access to world credit markets.

A lack of transparency

In the early 2000s, we invested in an Israeli pharmaceutical group with production facilities in low-cost countries and strong demand for its products in mature markets. We were in for the long haul.

We became uneasy when its results were late and wrote to the company asking for an explanation. We received no reply. The next we heard was that the company's CFO and a senior colleague had been sacked, but no explanation was given. Soon afterwards, the company was delisted by NASDAQ because it had not filed its annual report for the previous year. This was a serious blow because, without a listing, the market in the shares was limited and inefficient. We stuck it out, however, because the company seemed to have good growth prospects, strong products and an innovative track record.

A few months later, with the shares still in unlisted limbo, an Indian company made a tender offer for the shares, which the board recommended. The offer was pitched very low at what appeared to us to be a fire-sale price. Many investors feared the worst and took the money. The Indian group ended up in control, with almost half the shares and almost two-thirds of the voting rights. The company said its current board members were resigning, and that appointees of the Indian company would become directors in their stead.

We objected strongly to this proposal and another proposal to increase the professional indemnity cover for the departing board. We urged shareholders to reject the proposed indemnification and call for audited financial statements. We said the existing board of management had proved unable or unwilling to run the company in the interests of shareholders and did not deserve their support.

Other concerns were that the Israeli company's auditor had not been present at the meeting at which the merger had been approved and that, so far, the management had spent $40 million for professional and consulting fees to work on the audit.

Therefore, we and other investors rejected the offer and began a two-year legal campaign, demanding a full disclosure of the company's financial situation to the minority shareholders. The court found in our favour. The financial statements were disclosed, the tender offer was withdrawn and we accepted a new offer at twice the price of the original.

Carlos was in the thick of it all. 'I ran the whole thing,' he said, 'flying in and out of Tel Aviv on a regular basis; endless meetings with lawyers.' At the end of it all, one of the company's senior executives took him aside. 'Carlos,' he whispered, 'now that it's all over, let me tell you a thousand ways a pharma company can steal money from its shareholders.'

We never got to the bottom of what was really going on at the company, but for us, it was more than worth the time and effort to put up a fight for minority shareholder interests.

An activist generation

Not long ago, ordinary people, in their roles as consumers, workers and savers, were like Adam Smith's investors in the eighteenth century. They seldom 'pretended to understand anything of the business of the company', and received contentedly the goods and services they bought and the wage packets they earned. Labour unions used to be troublesome, but they seemed to be a spent force in most Western economies by the 1980s.

Today, companies are surrounded by activists of all kinds who refuse to buy from them or work for them if their behaviour on the ESG dimensions fails to meet basic standards. The millennials, and Generation Z (born in the mid-1990s) who follow them, have an ESG agenda, and woe betide companies that ignore it. In fact, when 'millennials' speak, it seems that even the mightiest in the corporate world tremble.

When Coca-Cola pledged in January 2018 to recycle all of its packaging by 2030, it was responding, not to an attack of corporate conscience, but to a conviction that continuing to take a cavalier attitude to the ultimate destiny of the 120 billion or so bottles it uses each year would be bad for business, and bad for the stock price (5.7).

It was a marketing decision, derived from the perception that the so-called 'millennial' generation had lost patience with the environmentally irresponsible packaging policies of consumer goods companies. The timing of the announcement might have had something to do with the then recent screening of *Blue Planet 2*, the latest instalment of Sir David Attenborough's oeuvre, in which the world-renowned British naturalist and film-maker had revealed the impact of plastic waste on marine life.

McDonald's also made a New Year's resolution: to make all its packaging from renewable or recyclable materials by 2025. The company said packaging was the most important environmental issue for its customers. Only 10 per cent of McDonald's restaurants worldwide currently offered recycling. McDonald's planned to raise that to 100 per cent by 2025. The UK frozen food retailer, Iceland, joined the New Year 2018 chorus, calling pollution a 'scourge', and promising to eliminate plastic packaging from its own-brand products by the end of 2023. Danone's water brand, Evian, has committed to making all of its bottles from recycled plastic by 2025.

Coca-Cola's CEO, James Quincey, also committed the company to making all its bottles with an average of 50 per cent recycled content by 2030. He said these new targets, announced on the eve of the World Economic Forum in Davos in 2018, would be an integral part of the group's business model. 'Consumers around the world care about our planet,' he told the *Financial Times*, 'and they want and expect companies to take action.' He urged other companies to make similar commitments on their packaging. Many already had.

Unilever has had a target of doubling its sales while halving its environmental footprint since 2010. It set itself another goal in 2017: to make all the plastic it uses recyclable, or reusable, by 2025. Procter & Gamble, Unilever's closest rival, has committed itself to ensuring 90 per cent of its packaging is recyclable by 2020. It offers discounts and coupons to encourage people to recycle, and supports investments in recycling facilities. Two other consumer goods groups, Nestlé and

Danone, teamed up in 2017 to develop a 'green' plastic bottle made from sawdust and cardboard.

In April 2018, more than 40 UK companies signed a UK Plastics Pact, pledging to strip unnecessary plastic from their shelves by 2025. Signatories included supermarket chains Sainsbury's, Tesco, Waitrose, Marks and Spencer and Morrisons, home delivery company Ocado, and consumer goods groups Unilever UK and Procter & Gamble UK. Together, they claimed to cover about 80 per cent of plastic packaging on UK supermarket shelves (5.8).

Since there are votes in environmental issues, politicians and governments are getting in on the act. In January 2018, UK Prime Minister Theresa May announced a target of eliminating avoidable plastic waste by 2042 (after the announcement of the ambitious UK Plastics Pact three months later, this seemed a relatively modest objective). The EU has pledged to ensure that, by 2030, the plastic packaging of all items sold within its borders will be recyclable.

Some question the validity of attributing these concerns to a particular generation, and argue that what has come to be seen as the millennial outlook is simply the zeitgeist. It is true that many people older and younger than millennials also watched and were moved by *Blue Planet 2*. Maybe so, but millennials are the largest generation and the main instruments of the zeitgeist. They are also a very large, multi-issue pressure group, who exert their pressure with the choices they make, as they adapt their behaviour to their outlooks and beliefs.

From the investor's point of view, the presence of this large millennial pressure group has three important implications. First, companies that supply goods and services, such as solar panels and 'reverse-vending' systems for plastic bottles (see p. 40), could do particularly well. Second, other things being equal, the company that is more responsive to multi-issue millennial pressures should be a better investment because it will attract more customers and more employees. Third, to identify the organisations most likely to be favoured by millennials, investors need ways to measure and assess the responsiveness of each organisation to this pressure.

If it is reasonable to attribute goals to a generation, which some dispute, we can say that in the companies they choose to work for, buy from and invest in, the millennials are putting pressure on companies to:

- become more environmentally and socially responsible, and more honest, straightforward, fair and open;
- honour their commitments in these areas;
- do these things at a reasonable cost so that millennials do not have to make significant sacrifices for them;
- do good in the world.

Words, deeds and evidence

In reaching their decisions about whether to buy from, work for or invest in one company and not another, or to vote for one political party and not another, millennials do not take declarations of good ESG intent at face value. They need evidence of the good behaviour promised by such declarations, just as ESG investors need evidence that the governance principles espoused by a company are reflected in the behaviour of its executives (see Chapter 7).

6

The investment continuum

There is no such thing as pure altruism. Everyone who gives, lends or invests does so in the expectation of a reward of some kind. A donor to a charity – an individual, a state, an NGO or a private organisation – earns a psychological return (the feeling of having done a good deed even when it is done anonymously), a reputational return (having been seen to have done a good deed) or both.

Charities and non-profits are purposeful organisations that identify needs that evoke compassion and deliver returns to their donors by satisfying those needs. They play an important role in emerging markets by helping to provide basic necessities such as clean water, healthcare, schools, housing, energy, roads and other infrastructural elements. The returns they deliver to their donors are psychological and consist of the positive feelings produced by the good the charities do for their beneficiaries.

By helping to meet basic needs, charities and non-profits active in emerging markets can also help to prepare the ground for other investors seeking more material returns.

Spectrum of capital

In 2012, the Spectrum of Capital chart was published by Bridges Ventures (now Bridges Fund Management), an organisation co-founded by Sir Ronald Cohen, a pioneer in social impact investment. It classified investors under headings ranging from 'philanthropic' (impact only) to 'traditional' (finance only). In between were four other types of emerging market investor. These formed what Bridges called 'The new paradigm':

1 *Philanthropy*: Impact only

2 *Impact first*: Impact, with some financial return

3 *Thematic*: Needs create opportunities for market-rate or market-beating returns

4 *Sustainable*: ESG opportunities through investment selection and shareholder advocacy

5 *Responsible*: ESG risk management, ranging from considering ESG factors to negative screening

6 *Traditional*: Finance only

These types refer to the different motivations and objectives of different investors. They should not be confused with the seven generic methodologies of ESG/sustainable investment identified by the GSIA and summarised as follows:

1 *Negative screening*: Excluding sectors, companies or business practices, according to ESG criteria

2 *Positive screening*: Including sectors, companies or projects on the basis of ESG criteria

3 *Norms screening*: Requiring investee firms to meet minimum ESG standards

4 *ESG integration*: Routinely including ESG factors in financial analysis

5 *Sustainability*: Investing in sustainable businesses in 'clean energy', green technology, sustainable agriculture, etc.

6 *Impact investing*: Investing in private markets to help solve social or environmental problems

7 *Corporate engagement*: Exerting influence by talking to senior managers and boards, filing motions and proxy voting, guided by ESG principles

There is some overlap between the two lists, in that the use of a methodology can help define a particular investor's objective or motivation. For example, a characteristic approach of 'sustainable' investors, which is where we locate ourselves on the Bridges spectrum, is 'corporate engagement' or shareholder advocacy.

Let us look at this 'new paradigm' of investors, beginning with 'impact first' investors.

Impact first

The new kid on the ESG investment block is 'impact' investing, the GSIA's sixth category of ESG investing (see Chapter 1). It is new, not in the sense that it has not been done before, but in the sense that it has only recently been given a name. The term is said to have been coined in 2007, at a conference held at the Rockefeller Foundation's Bellagio Centre on the shores of Lake Como in northern Italy. It was used to describe investment that seeks measurable social and environmental benefits as well as a financial return.

Amit Bouri, CEO of the Global Impact Investing Network (GIIN) and a tireless evangelist for impact investing, attributes much of the recent rapid growth of the impact segment of the market to the naming, which, he says, 'connected a bunch of really exciting, [but] fragmented efforts into a unified market' (6.1).

The motivation of the impact investor is to change things for the better, without losing his or her shirt. In the Bridges model, philanthropy, where the investor seeks no financial return or any repayment of the principal, is called 'impact only'. What most of us understand by the term 'impact investing' is Bridges' 'impact first' category, where there is an expectation of some financial as well as an impact return. According to the UK's National Advisory Board on Impact Investing, 'impact first' would include: 'backing social business models that re-invest some, or all their financial surpluses'.

Most of the recent commitments to impact investing by various funds and foundations have been of the 'impact first' kind.

In December 2017, the $12 billion Ford Foundation announced that it had recruited Roy Swan, from Morgan Stanley, to run its $1 billion fund earmarked for 'mission' or 'impact' investing. Swan's task was to produce 'social' as well as market returns to reflect the belief of the Ford Foundation's trustees that there is more to modern philanthropy than giving. As Darren Walker, Ford Foundation's

President, told a *Financial Times* conference: 'It's not just the 5 per cent of your money you give away that matters. What you do with the other 95 per cent is almost more important' (6.2).

Other charities, including the Rockefeller Foundation and the Bill & Melinda Gates Foundation, are also committing funds to the new 'impact' investing sector and, at the 2017 World Economic Forum, UBS 'pledged to direct $5 billion of our clients' investments over the next five years to sustainable or impact investments'. In choosing its sustainable investments, UBS was being guided by the UN's 17 Sustainable Development Goals (SDGs) that aim to end poverty, protect the planet and bring prosperity to all by 2030 (see box, below).

UNITED NATIONS SUSTAINABLE DEVELOPMENT GOALS

Goal 1: No poverty

Goal 2: Zero hunger

Goal 3: Good health and well-being

Goal 4: Quality education

Goal 5: Gender equality

Goal 6: Clean water and sanitation

Goal 7: Affordable and clean energy

Goal 8: Decent work and economic growth

Goal 9: Industry, innovation and infrastructure

Goal 10: Reduced inequalities

Goal 11: Sustainable cities and communities

Goal 12: Responsible consumption and production

Goal 13: Climate action

Goal 14: Life below water

Goal 15: Life on land

Goal 16: Peace, justice and strong institutions

Goal 17: Partnerships for the Goals

Source: United Nations.

Impact investing is intimately linked to these SDGs, which were agreed at a UN summit in 2015. The SDGs have played a particularly important role in impact investing in emerging markets because it is to the SDGs that impact investors look in order to identify areas where impact is needed.

Impact Summit Europe, an annual investor conference on impact investing organised by investment consultants, Phenix Capital, is squarely focused on the UN's SDGs. Phenix's declared vision is 'to contribute to a better world by closing the SDG financing gap'. It says its goal is to help large signatories to the UN PRI (see p. 17) 'to allocate up to 5% of their assets to impact investments', and thus 'direct $800 billion to the SDGs over the next decade' (6.3).

The latest biennial survey, published by the GIIN (see above) in 2017, estimated that about $114 billion had been committed to impact investing. The GSIA says 'impact investing' is the fastest-growing 'sustainable' investment strategy. It is hard to be sure about these figures because some of the investing alleged to be 'impact' or 'mission' investing is little more than 'negative screening': the exclusion from portfolios of non-ESG-compliant and 'sin' stocks (tobacco, alcohol, arms, etc.). It seems fair to say, however, that, although impact investing only accounts for a couple of percentage points of total professionally managed assets, it is on a high-growth trajectory.

The African Investing for Impact Barometer, maintained by the Bertha Centre for Social Innovation and Entrepreneurship at the University of Cape Town's Graduate School of Business, covers the GSIA's methodologies of ESG integration, corporate engagement and positive, negative and norms-based screening in its research. The barometer focuses on South Africa, Nigeria and Kenya, the three largest economies in sub-Saharan Africa. ESG integration and corporate engagement are most prevalent in South Africa and Kenya, and corporate governance plays the largest ESG role in investment decision-making. South African asset managers are more open about ESG integration and corporate engagement than their counterparts in Kenya and Nigeria, probably because South Africa's largest asset managers have signed up to the UN PRI (see p. 17). 'Negative' screening is the dominant form of screening in the three countries, where private equity and venture funds are guided by the International Finance Corporation's standards, particularly in screening out 'sin' stocks (6.4).

In addition to problems of definition, 'impact' investing also struggles with measurement problems. It is hard to say an 'impact' fund is underperforming, for instance, if it has chosen to favour hard-to-measure 'social' over 'financial' returns.

For example, one of the Ford Foundation's initial impact investments is in 'affordable housing' in Detroit and Newark in the USA. This project exemplifies the inherent tension in impact investing between ESG and financial returns: both kinds of return will clearly depend on the 'affordability' of the housing – the higher the ESG return, the lower the financial return.

However, if a balance is struck between social and financial returns, a financial component in the return is *sine qua non*, or a defining characteristic, of impact investing. In April 2018, a Swedish professor who is a prominent lobbyist for impact investing came to see us. To distance our new company from impact investing, we explained that we were strictly profit-orientated. Our visitor was outraged. 'Never say that again,' she pleaded. 'Impact investing is always profit-orientated.'

The crucial difference between philanthropy (impact only) and the Bridges 'impact-first' category is that the former focuses on needs, while the latter focuses on the means to address them. The financial component of the return is essential because without it, the means, usually a company, will not be 'sustainable'. The value of impact investing for emerging market countries is that it helps them to reduce their dependence on 'the kindness of strangers'.

Jacqueline Novogratz, the founder and CEO of Acumen, one of a new breed of dedicated impact investors, talks of 'patient capital' (i.e. long-term capital), as distinct from grants or gifts. As a former international credit analyst at Chase Manhattan Bank, she is well aware of the problem of measurement. She and her colleagues have devoted a considerable effort to developing their 'Lean Data' methodology (see p. 170).

Acumen supports various sectors, including agriculture, water and sanitation, education, health, housing and energy. It invests in entrepreneurs with good ideas about how to address local needs because it believes that, although it is slower than satisfying the needs directly, it is more cost efficient, more sustainable and 'can change overall systems. Forever' (6.5).

In her foreword to Acumen's *Energy Impact Report*, Novogratz invites the reader to 'Imagine a life without electricity,' a life led by one in seven people today. It means, 'spending 10% of your income on kerosene ... inhaling fumes equivalent to smoking two packs of cigarettes a day ... spending hours searching for firewood to cook each meal'.

Novogratz believes that, thanks in part to the 80 per cent fall in the price of solar panels in recent years, Africa, 'which still has 600 million people living without electricity', has an opportunity to 'solve its energy problem with ... affordable solar power and leapfrog the electrical grid altogether'.

She sees Acumen as occupying a place on a continuum and as an incubator of companies that may later attract 'a wider spectrum of investors'. In the Bridges model, Acumen would rank as 'impact first', in that impact takes priority over financial return. This is the category most people understand by the term 'impact investing'. Two further points need to be made about this kind of investment. The first is that, since 'impact' is an output, the success of such investments cannot be measured in terms of inputs but, as already noted, output in these areas is very hard to measure (see Chapter 7). It is easy to measure the cost of building a school, for example, but hard to measure its impact on standards of education. The second point is that, partly because of these measurement challenges and partly because innovative start-ups and small and medium-sized firms have a key role to play in meeting the SDGs, impact investing in public markets is still in its infancy.

Before moving on to other Bridges categories, let us consider a particular kind of investment that looks like philanthropy from one angle but more like 'impact first' from another.

Pro bono

David Ogilvy, founder of the Ogilvy & Mather advertising agency, was in the habit of walking across Central Park to his Madison Avenue office each morning. Each day, he passed a beggar with a sign round his neck, which informed passers-by he was 'BLIND'. Ogilvy did not believe in giving money to beggars, but on one fine April morning, his conscience pricked him. He took the sign from the beggar's neck, edited the notice with a felt-tip pen so it read, 'IT IS SPRING AND I AM BLIND,' and replaced it. Legend has it that by noon, the beggar's cup was overflowing.

The idea that gifts of time by people with talent, skills and experience can be as valuable to deprived communities as gifts of money, naturally leads to the 'volunteering' element of CSR programmes being imported into ESG-linked 'impact' investing. Business services firm EY (formerly Ernst & Young) calls it 'impact entrepreneurship'. It gives the time of its professionals to help businesses all over the world with planning, execution and general business development. Whether or not a particular business is offered help by EY depends on whether it is contributing to the UN's SDGs (see box, p. 141).

In its *Scaling Impact Entrepreneurship 2017* yearbook, EY gives a dozen examples of its impact entrepreneur work in 2017. AccuHealth is a Chilean telemedicine service that is making it easier for patients to obtain medical advice and to manage chronic conditions at home. EY professionals helped the company to enter the Mexican and Colombian markets as early steps towards its goal of serving a million customers by 2020. The business was judged to be contributing to the third, eighth and seventeenth UN SDGs.

Talian is a family-run, African agri-business, specialising in maize and cassava milling. With investment from Africa Agriculture Development Company, backed by the UK Department for International Development (DfID) and EY help with its financial and operational controls, Talian aims to increase the scale of its operations sixfold in five years, 'creating hundreds of skilled jobs and linking thousands of small-scale farmers to export and premium markets'. EY says that the business contributes to the first, second, eighth and seventeenth UN SDGs.

Husk Power Systems provides rural communities with affordable power from renewable sources. It plans to add more than 300 mini-grids in India and Tanzania in the next four years, serving 65,000 homes and small businesses. EY has helped the company to design an organisation structure and an IT system that can accommodate these ambitious growth plans. The business was deemed to be contributing to the first, seventh and eighth UN SDGs.

M-KOPA is similar to Husk Power Systems but uses a different source of energy. It has already connected more than half a million homes to solar power in East Africa. With EY's help in streamlining its operations and reducing the costs of customer support, it aims to reach 3 million of Kenya's 5 million off-grid households by 2025, so helping them to save substantial fuel costs. The business contributes to the first, seventh and eighth UN SDGs.

The impact here is the improved performance of firms assisted by EY's professionals. But there are also other returns that have financial value for EY, such as the personal development of staff and network and reputational gains. And it is also easy to see how the EY programme could be usefully combined with more conventional impact-first investments, and thus make them more attractive to 'a wider spectrum of investors'.

From impact to ESG

The third category in the Bridges spectrum is 'thematic': the investor selects a few SDG-related issues such as clean energy, healthcare and microfinance, and then invests in companies making an impact in these areas, with the intention of earning market-rate or market-beating returns. Bridges sees 'thematic' as part of the high-impact segment of the spectrum because, like impact only and impact first, its target selection is based on the SDGs.

After 'thematic' comes Bridges' 'sustainable' category. This is where ESG takes over from SDG-related 'impact' as the basis of stock selection. A 'sustainable' strategy seeks ESG opportunities through investment selection, portfolio management and shareholder advocacy This is the segment of the Bridges spectrum where we are operating (see below). Sustainable differs from the next category, 'responsible', because it is 'active'. Responsible is focused on ESG risks rather than opportunities; it is a 'passive' strategy, which employs negative ESG screening as its main selection method.

The Bridges spectrum ends with 'traditional' investing, which is entirely focused on financial returns and gives no more than a distant nod in the direction of ESG.

Traditional impact

The Bridges Spectrum of Capital is a useful framework for thinking about the different motivations of investors in emerging markets. There is an implication here, however, that not all companies with the potential to have a substantial beneficial impact on emerging markets should be backed by the Bridges 'high-impact' strategies of philanthropy, impact first and thematic. This is because, like philanthropists, impact-first and thematic investors, with limited resources, should be focused on needs not being met by other types of investor.

In other words, there is a contradiction embedded in the impact-investing idea. Impact investors, which require financial returns, should steer clear of high-impact businesses offering market-rate or better returns because they should have no trouble in attracting capital from more conventional investors. 'Impact' funds should be reserved for companies and projects that would not attract capital from traditional investors.

This division of labour is not strictly adhered to in emerging markets because markets are less than perfectly efficient and capital markets, for business start-ups and small and medium-sized enterprises, are particularly inefficient in emerging markets.

But in addition to having more pressing needs than the mature markets and so offering more potential for generating SDG-related impact returns, rapidly growing emerging markets will also include listed investment opportunities that are attractive to traditional investors.

The ESG and SDG benefits of such investments are incidental but they can, nonetheless, be substantial.

Microfinance

We have invested in a microfinance holding company listed on the Botswana Stock Exchange. It makes very small, short- to medium-term unsecured loans of $10–100 to over 300,000 customers, most of whom are women, through subsidiaries in ten countries in Africa.

The company helps people living in remote villages, to set up businesses selling SIM cards, for instance, or cooking equipment and fresh produce. It stimulates company formation, which creates more jobs, and helps women to become financially independent. With over 2,300 staff, the group is a big employer in its own right. Demonstrating the potential for 'leap-frogging' the stages of development in emerging markets, it uses mobile phones and bespoke apps to manage the accounts of customers who lack, and have little prospect of acquiring, conventional bank accounts.

It is a big success story. The company has grown fast, by acquisition as well as organically. It is profitable, and therefore sustainable, and, in areas where it operates, indigenous corporate sectors are growing strongly, albeit from a low base. In other words, it's delivering substantial social benefits to its customers as well as solid financial returns to its investors.

M-Pesa

Another example of such 'leap-frogging' related to microfinance is M-Pesa (M for mobile and pesa for 'money' in Swahili). This phone-based payment, financing and microfinancing service was launched in 2007 by Vodafone for its associates, Safaricom and Vodacom, market-leading network operators in Kenya and Tanzania, respectively.

The system is simple. Customers take money to M-Pesa-licensed shops and give it to registered agents. The agents generate codes with Vodafone's code generator, which they then give to customers, in exchange for the cash. Customers text the codes to whoever they want. The recipient takes the code to the local M-Pesa shop and exchanges it for the cash specified. Users are charged a small fee for sending and withdrawing money.

By the end of its first year in 2008, M-Pesa had 1.2 million customers and was on a steep growth trajectory. Ten years later, it was serving nearly 30 million customers through a network of over 287,400 agents. In 2016, the service handled 6 billion transactions at a peak rate of 529 a second.

Such an elegant system! It is successful because it has taken into account Africa's basic infrastructure and the lack of regulations, which, in mature markets, would have made it difficult to offer such a service to the public. Although it was born in Africa and was developed by Africans, the system has qualities suited to emerging markets everywhere. Through its local associates, Vodafone offers the service in ten countries, including Albania, India and Romania (see box below).

THE ORIGINS OF M-PESA

THE SCIENCE-FICTION NOVELIST William Gibson's suggestion that 'the street finds its own uses for technology' was neatly corroborated in 2002 by research at UK technology transfer company Gamos, and the Commonwealth Telecommunications Organisation.

During a study funded by the UK's DfID, of mobile phone use in sub-Saharan Africa, the researchers found mobile phone airtime was being routinely used as a private currency. People were transferring their airtime credits to friends and relatives, who were then using or reselling them.

Gamos researchers approached Mcel, Mozambique's first mobile operator, with an idea. In 2004, Mcel introduced the first official airtime credit barter exchange.

The idea was discussed by the Commission for Africa, and the DfID introduced the researchers to UK operator Vodafone, which had been thinking about ways to support microfinance and banking services with mobile phones. Gamos and Vodafone discussed the creation of a mobile-based money transfer system in Kenya. A student at Kenya's Moi University developed an app that allowed mobile users to send, receive and withdraw money with their mobiles. Safaricom, Vodafone's Kenyan associate, bought the rights to the app from the student and, in April 2007, launched M-Pesa.

The service is doing well financially, and also doing good. A paper written by economists Tavneet Suri of MIT and William Jack of Georgetown University, about M-Pesa's impact on Kenya, appeared in *Science* in December 2016 (6.6). Their research, part-funded by the Bill & Melinda Gates Foundation, found that access to M-Pesa services in Kenya since 2008 had increased per capita consumption and lifted some 194,000 Kenyan households out of 'extreme poverty' (living on less than $1.25 a day). Female-led households saw much greater increases in consumption than male-led households. It has been estimated that mobile-money services have helped some 185,000 Kenyan women move from farming to business occupations.

By allowing users to deposit, withdraw or transfer money and pay for goods and services with mobile phones, M-Pesa weakens the business case for conventional financial services delivery systems and allows emerging markets to leap-frog the branch-based stage of banking development. More importantly, it has made cheap financial services available to millions of people previously locked out of the conventional banking system either because their credit was no good, they were too poor or because they either did not know how or were afraid to approach a conventional bank.

For external investors, who own 25 per cent and 21 per cent, respectively, of Safaricom and Vodacom, M-Pesa delivers a strong tick in the social element of ESG. Through their impacts on entrepreneurial activity and company formation in the countries in which they operate, our microfinance company and M-Pesa are helping to create investment opportunities attractive to conventional investors. In effect, they are helping to re-rate the emerging markets where they are active.

They share another distinctive feature – they generate strong financial as well as excellent psychological returns. The one type of return does not compromise the other. Financial returns fuel the psychological returns. They make the organisations self-sufficient and thus 'sustainable', which makes them exemplary investments for the ESG age.

Our place on the spectrum of capital

As we said above, we see ourselves in the 'sustainable' segment of the Bridges spectrum. We seek ESG opportunities through careful investment selection. We manage our portfolio actively and develop relationships with the managements and boards of the companies we invest in. In the event of disagreements and disputes, we exercise our rights, as minority shareholders to challenge a board, in the courts if necessary, we suspect of acting against the interests of all shareholders.

Whenever possible, we will make common cause with other minority investors.

Our role is similar to EY's 'impact entrepreneurship', in that it often involves an element of teaching. We are not 'volunteers', imparting knowledge about management and technology on a pro bono basis. However, by making our views on governance issues known to the companies we invest in, we are teaching them how to plug into the world economy and attract foreign capital. We are dissimilar from EY's programme, of course, in that we seek a financial as well as an ESG return.

Another point to note is that we and other 'sustainable' (in the Bridges sense) investors are the gatekeepers of, and access points to, the world's mobile pool of capital, which is constantly seeking higher financial and, increasingly, ESG returns.

We are the infantry of the wider spectrum of investors. We see the companies we invest in, face to face; not as abstractions with ESG labels, but as real enterprises, on the ground, each with its own style, colours, noises, smells and ambience. The bigger funds do not stock-pick in emerging markets. To adapt their portfolios to the outlook of their beneficiaries, they buy packages of ESG stuff by backing activist ESG investors and tracking ESG indices.

To reflect the growing interest of asset owners worldwide in ESG – as noted in Chapter 1, about 26 per cent ($23 trillion) of all assets managed globally were ESG-screened in one way or another in 2016, according to the GSIA – ESG 'technology' has evolved from the simple negative screening of so-called 'sin' stocks, into a more sophisticated, data-hungry set of tools and analytical techniques. Positive screening has become more popular. 'Carbon-footprint' reduction commitments (in which the Japanese government's enormous, $1.3 trillion pension fund is particularly interested) are now commonplace and full integration of ESG factors in fundamental analysis has become more widespread.

This has been accompanied by demands for more transparent and accurate ESG reporting, which emerging market companies, with less rigorous reporting and disclosure requirements, often find it hard to comply with. And this, in turn, has led to the perception that, in general, emerging market firms are not as ESG-compliant as their developed market peers.

Egon Vavrek, an emerging markets portfolio manager at Dutch pension fund managers APG, says this does emerging markets firms an injustice. 'If we compare corporates in the same sector, of the same size (small-cap data quality is still somewhat subpar), we do not find systemically poorer scores for emerging market companies than for developed market ones,' he wrote in the *Financial Times* in July 2017 (6.7).

He sees signs of improvement in some emerging markets, 'where regulators, [stock] exchanges and corporates have come together to establish fairly advanced reporting standards'. He cited the 2010 introduction in South Africa of the Johannesburg Stock Exchange's Integrated Reporting Standards. 'As corporates implemented these standards and their disclosure improved ... their ranking and scores within sustainability providers' databases also improved.' Vavrek said that most of these improvements came from better data quality and disclosure rather than improvements in the way companies were complying with ESG criteria.

According to Vavrek, the problem is that too many large funds are unwilling to invest in gathering raw data in emerging markets and prefer to rely on simple, 'easy to digest' scoring systems for judging sustainability.

When Japan's state pension fund announced its decision to put more emphasis on low-carbon outcomes in its investing, it bemoaned the fact that most environmental stock indices were assembled by excluding some industries rather than including 'green' companies that actively contributed to sustainable environment. The managers invited 'proposals for global environmental stock indices' (6.8).

We will look in more detail at ESG measurement and indices in emerging markets in Chapter 7. For the moment, it is sufficient to note that, although there are signs of improvement in data-gathering and analysis in emerging markets, a deeper trend is taking a growing proportion of investment funds beyond the reach of emerging market companies: the lack of data, and of indices with enough resolution to reflect reality accurately at the corporate level, are denying emerging market companies access to the large and rapidly growing proportions of equity and bond funds managed passively.

There is no mystery about why passively managed tracker funds have grabbed almost half the market. They are cheaper. Because they do not have to spend much on research and analysis, they can charge lower management fees. But in setting themselves up to be low-cost, they are effectively abnegating the investor's governance role of holding company management teams to account (see Chapter 3).

The big passive fund management companies come under pressure from time to time, for instance when they failed to reduce their holdings in gun manufacturers after the killing of 17 students at the Marjory Stoneman Douglas High School in Parkland, Florida, in February 2018. Several large passive funds have said they want to become more responsive, but they have dispensed with the means to do so. Their business models are based on economies of scale, not on how effectively they and 'proxy advisers', such as ISS and Glass Lewis to which they delegate their oversight role, discharge their governance responsibilities.

It is a problem for all markets, but particularly for emerging markets, where vigilant and active investors are required to push and prod companies to improve their ESG performance.

As we acknowledged in Chapter 1, the ESG screening provided by passively managed Exchange Traded Funds that track ESG indices is much better than nothing. When all is said and done, however, its ability to separate the ESG wheat from the chaff is limited by the relative lack of raw data and the consequently lower resolution of currently available ESG indices.

ESG indices for emerging markets will improve, but until they do, there will be no substitute for active investing.

Corporate colonialism

The other kind of investor in emerging markets, quite separate from the Bridges spectrum, are the multinational companies that invest in or start local associates or subsidiaries. M-Pesa's pioneers, Safaricom in Kenya, and Vodacom in neighbouring Tanzania, are good examples of such corporate colonialism. Both are associates of the UK-based global mobile phone operator, Vodafone.

The importance of such businesses to emerging markets is that they bring a lot of baggage with them, in the form of their parent companies' cultures, missions, strategies, processes, experience, organisation structures, values, best practices and ways of doing things. Many of these imports, including the people who bring them and apply them, are useful to emerging markets because they teach local people about Western standards of management and governance.

Mark remembers visiting the Nigerian subsidiary of SAB Miller (formerly South African Breweries and now part of AB Inbev). 'They had a beautiful set-up,' he recalled. 'They were carrying on all of the SAB practices, including the way they treated employees.'

We invested in an SAB brewery in Zimbabwe, of all places. The government was in turmoil, public finances were collapsing because the government was running out of dollars and capital flight had reached critical levels. On the face of it, therefore, investing in any Zimbabwean company at the time was the height of folly.

But, despite all this turbulence and dysfunction, our brewery (rated the cleanest in Africa) was doing extremely well. The share price quadrupled in two years because local investors were buying the stock. They trusted foreign-owned companies such as SAB more than their local companies because they had more faith in their management expertise and track records. SAB's reputation as one of the world's most efficient brewers added to the perceived value of the stock.

However, in addition to this copying-and-pasting of standards from the parent company, there is a less desirable parental tendency to neglect the interests of co-investors. They have de facto control. They take all the decisions at shareholder meetings and decide all business and operational issues. They run the business itself well enough, but some of their corporate governance standards in areas such as disclosure and investor relations are weak. When managing subsidiaries or associates in emerging markets, some foreign parent companies use their de facto control more for the benefit of their own investors than for those of the subsidiary or associate. Dividend policy may be less generous than that of the parent, for instance, or, for tax reasons, management may be under instructions from the parent to 'manage' the profitability of a subsidiary or associate in ways that are to the detriment of minority shareholders and the local economies. Common practices here include 'transfer-pricing' arrangements, designed to move profits to low-tax jurisdictions, onerous central management services fees and exorbitant royalties for the use of brand names.

According to the African Development Bank (ADB), Africa loses about $60 billion a year 'in illicit financial [out]flows, through trade under-invoicing, transfer pricing by multinational companies, and corruption' (6.9). Under-invoicing, moving money illicitly across borders by under-stating the value of exports on customs invoices, is the largest single kind of illicit financial outflow measured by the pressure group Global Financial Integrity (GFI). It's used for money laundering, tax and customs duty evasion, bogus claims for tax incentives, and dodging capital controls. Transfer pricing (prices charged in intra-firm transactions) is tightly regulated in Western tax jurisdictions, but abusive practices, including the over-billing, by foreign parents, for central services supplied to local subsidiaries, are still common in emerging markets.

Orange Polska, as discussed in detail in Chapter 5, is a case in point.

Despite the sometimes predatory attitude of multinationals to emerging markets, on balance we believe that, for developing economies, the benefits of their subsidiaries and associates outweigh the costs. They treat developing countries as developing countries and do not always fully apply their ESG policies. But, by taking market share away from the informal breweries that had traditionally been the main suppliers of beer in emerging markets, for example, SAB's subsidiaries have brought brewing within the tax net and may also have reduced the health risks associated with illicit brewing.

When investing in what are usually seen as 'sin' stocks, such as breweries and tobacco companies, there are always issues about whether they are ESG compliant, and the risks that governments will impose taxes or restrictions on advertising. When we were thinking of investing in a Kenyan brewer, we were told not to worry about all that because the brewer was on the side of the angels. Without it, Kenyans would be worse off.

There is a long tradition of home-brewing in many African countries and, recently, we were told, it had become the thing among home brewers to toss used batteries into the 'mash' to give the beer an 'electric' flavour. But ordinary, 'dry' batteries consist of chemicals such as zinc, manganese dioxide, ammonium and zinc chlorides and potassium hydroxide, most of which are slightly to highly toxic. 'People have died from it,' we were told. Beer produced by regulated breweries is much healthier because it uses clean water and has a lower alcohol content.

These nauseating stories of batteries in home-brewed mash may have been the hyperbole of the brewery's public relations people. But you do not have to be a credulous PR pushover to believe that the interests of local public health will be served if regulated breweries, with modern equipment and technology, high standards of hygiene and lower prices, drive out the home-brewers.

7

Measurement and performance

There is no doubt in our minds that the 'new paradigm' investors in Bridges Fund Management's Spectrum of Capital (see Chapter 6) have created, and are continuing to create, a great deal of ESG value, and are having a substantial beneficial impact both on the countries where they operate, and on the planet.

The new paradigm players differ from the traditional investor and philanthropist in seeking two kinds of return – a conventional financial return; and an unconventional, psychological return that is related to the environmental, social and governance performance of a portfolio company, or to its contribution to meeting the UN's 17 SDGs.

But it is one thing to be confident that good is being done by the new paradigm investors and quite another to know precisely, or even roughly, how much good they are doing.

Setting aside various complications related to the structures of multinational groups and to transfer pricing arrangements, it is easy enough to measure the financial component of a company's or a portfolio's return. But what of the non-financial component? This is important information because, without it, there is no way to assess the performance of a new paradigm fund relative to that of other new paradigm funds or to conventionally managed funds.

As we have said more than once, measuring ESG performance by its non-financial outcomes is one of the major challenges facing new paradigm investors. Right now, companies and funds are in transition mode and declaring their allegiance to ESG with promises of reform and compliance with the ESG gospel. Before long, ESG will be a settled fixture of the investment environment, and attention will shift from whether or not companies and managed funds are committed to ESG principles to how much ESG bang they are getting from their ESG bucks.

To put this point another way, until recently a commitment to ESG was a 'differentiation' criterion: it made the company or fund stand out. Today it is fast becoming a 'qualification' criterion: a necessary condition for the right to compete.

In this chapter, we will look at some of the problems with the measurement of non-financial returns and some suggested solutions. We will then address the question with which we began the book: 'Is there money in it?' Can ESG investing, 'active' ESG investing, and 'active' ESG investing in emerging markets, deliver market-rate or better financial returns?

We want to emphasise yet again that the two-pack return, part financial, part non-financial, is an integral part of the business model of new paradigm investors. It is what distinguishes them from charities at one end of the spectrum and conventional investors at the other. In our view, it is a source of great strength because it can make doing good self-financing, and therefore 'sustainable'.

If it turns out that new paradigm investors can do good in an ESG or SDG sense *and* enjoy market rate or better financial returns at the same time, they could change the world.

Measuring by proxy

If, over a period of a few years, 100,000 women in an African country where employment patterns have remained unchanged since time immemorial, leave their family farms and set up their own businesses, you can be fairly sure that something important in the local environment has changed. But what?

Is it the introduction of more efficient farming methods, the arrival of smartphone payments systems, the improvement of roads, a strengthening of property rights or the start of state provision of education for women fifteen years earlier? It is possible that it is a combination of all these things, and of more besides: that these hitherto separate developments suddenly coalesced and precipitated a major phase transition in the way women saw the world, and their places in it.

This is the problem with measuring non-financial returns – it is very hard and often impossible to link causes to effects. For want of more precise measures, therefore, those concerned with ESG issues, including consumers and employees as well as new paradigm investors, have to make use of proxy variables.

One such proxy are the announcements by consumer goods groups of commitments to adopt more environmentally responsible packaging policies. As we mentioned in Chapter 5, Coca-Cola shares became more attractive to ESG investors after its pledge in January 2018 to collect and recycle all its packaging by 2030. Investors knew Coca-Cola products and jobs would thereby become more attractive to millennials.

But promises are cheap. Knowledgeable investors will not be persuaded by declarations of intent. They will want and expect their fund managers to demand clear evidence of action and progress towards ESG targets and objectives, to keep an active watch on the ESG performance of portfolio companies and act on evidence of improvement or backsliding.

Research in 2015 by the Ellen MacArthur Foundation – set up by Dame Ellen MacArthur after her solo circumnavigation of the globe to promote environmentally friendly business models – found that 40 years after the introduction of the universal recycling symbol on packaging, only 14 per cent of such packaging was separately collected and barely 2 per cent was actually recycled. In other words, despite heightened popular sensitivity to the man-made problem of long-lived plastic waste, very little was being done about it at the time of the MacArthur Foundation's research. The large number of new company commitments at the end of 2017 and early 2018 in the wake of the *Blue Planet 2* screening suggested that companies were at last beginning to take the issue seriously. But whether this was a genuine inflection point or another false dawn remains to be seen.

A recent development, or more accurately, a revival of an old practice, from a time when packaging was expensive, is the idea of incentives for returning 'empties'. P&G is offering discounts and coupons to encourage recycling. Coca-Cola is considering a 'scan-and-win programme', in which consumers of its products are entered in a prize draw if they return bottles. As reported in Chapter 2, a Chinese company we have invested in makes and operates so-called 'reverse-vending' machines (see p. 40). Such schemes cost money and this suggests that the companies using them may, indeed, be taking their recycling commitments seriously.

Offering incentives to encourage scavenging and returning the scavenged waste to the supplier is a potentially very powerful recycling stimulus, but it begs some questions for the ESG investor. How much of an incentive is needed to change consumer behaviour? Is the intrinsic value of the waste sufficient to cover the costs of incentives, collection and cleaning? If it is not, how will the required subsidy or price premium affect financial returns? Is the non-financial return of less discarded waste – a feeling of having contributed to a cleaner planet – enough in an ESG investor's view to offset any reduction in financial return? ESG investors might conclude that they would prefer the waste producer to spend the money required to finance behaviour-changing subsidies on reducing their use of packaging in the first place.

In making such judgements, ESG investors will need to consider the unpriced 'externalities' (the incidental impact on unrelated third parties, see Chapter 2) of waste recycling such as reduced carbon emissions, cleaner public spaces and less leaching of plastic microparticles into our rivers and oceans. Ultimately, each ESG investor and consumer must make up his or her own mind. Their different priorities will lead to different trade-offs. All will require information, however, on corporate practices and the provenance of goods.

The monitors

Direct guidance for ESG investors is provided by a variety of indices and rankings that monitor the ESG credentials of companies and the funds that invest in them.

Sustainalytics, for example, rates the 'sustainability' of listed companies according to their ESG performance. It is based in Amsterdam in the Netherlands, and was created by the merger of Toronto-based Jantzi Research, founded in 1992, and its European counterpart. In 2000, it launched the Jantzi Social Index, the first socially screened stock index for Canadian listed companies. In 2013, it rolled out the Global Compact 100 index in partnership with the 'United Nations Global Compact', a 13,000-strong group of companies committed to ten principles of sustainability and social responsibility.

It has carved out an influential niche for itself in ESG investment because of the quality of its analysis and its record in spotting trends and issues early. It expressed concerns about governance at Volkswagen months before the emissions scandal broke in 2015, and issued similar warnings about governance at Fiat Automobiles 18 months before the Italian carmaker was accused of breaking emissions laws in 104,000 diesel vehicles in early 2017.

In 2015, the *Harvard Business Review* gave Sustainalytics its much-prized imprimatur by including its ESG Rating in its assessment of the 100 best-performing CEOs in the world. The STOXX Global ESG Leaders Index uses Sustainalytics data to help identify best-in-class stocks.

In 2016, Morningstar, a Chicago-based investment research and management company, released the first sustainability rankings for mutual and Exchange Traded Funds (ETFs). Scores were calculated by applying Sustainalytics' research to the companies in each fund's portfolio. The following year, Morningstar acquired a 40 per cent stake in Sustainalytics.

In 2017, ING Group issued the first loan of which the coupon is coupled to the sustainability rating of the lender, Koninklijke Philips N.V., as measured by Sustainalytics.

MSCI Inc., a leading index formulator, offers a family of ESG indices, from which ETFs can derive ESG credentials. For example, MSCI's ACWI [All Country World Index] Sustainable Impact Index is made up of companies that derive 50 per cent or more of their revenue from products or services that support the UN's SDGs (see p. 141).

The Thomson Reuters Corporate Responsibility indices are also designed to measure the ESG performance of companies.

MSCI also rates corporate bonds according to their exposures 'to industry-specific ESG risks and their ability to manage those risks relative to peers'. It covers 6,400 companies and a total of 11,800 issuers, including subsidiaries.

In June 2013, Barclays Bank and MSCI joined forces to launch a family of fixed-income indices based on ESG criteria, which they hoped would stimulate sustainable investing in bond markets.

Institutional Shareholder Services (ISS) advises investors on corporate governance issues. It offers 'a suite of ESG solutions' to help investors to 'develop and integrate responsible investing policies and practices into their strategy, and execute upon these policies through end-to-end voting'.

In recent years, regulatory authorities around the world have had to come to terms with the hunger of modern investors for ESG-screened securities. In 2008, the US pensions regulator warned fund managers that the Employee Retirement Income Security Act (ERISA), which protects pension assets with rules that qualified plans must abide by, obliged them not to allow ESG screening to distract them from their fiduciary duty to maximise financial returns. But seven years later, the language of US officialdom had softened. In 2015, the US Department of Labor said that it did not believe ERISA rules precluded ESG screening. In the same year, the French government passed a law that made ESG and climate-change reporting compulsory for public companies, banks and institutional investors.

Today's ESG investment space is also populated by a number of forums, think tanks and talking shops that are collectively adding to our knowledge, flagging problems and issues, raising awareness and setting standards. In a 2011 report, for example, the European Sustainable Investment Forum (Eurosif) said only 42 per cent of companies in emerging markets supported the adoption of sustainable policies and were generally less diligent than their counterparts in mature markets in implementing them. At that time, Chinese companies were seen as poor in labour relations and corruption, and Russian companies were particularly weak in governance.

The International Integrated Reporting Council (IIRC) aims to drag financial reporting into the ESG age. It is a global coalition of regulators, investors, companies, standard setters, accountancy firms and NGOs that bills a holistic concept of value creation as the next step in the evolution of corporate reporting.

The IIRC vision is 'to align capital allocation and corporate behaviour to wider goals of financial stability and sustainable development through ... integrated reporting and thinking'. To this end, it has produced an 'International <IR> Framework'. At the time of writing, it was market testing the <IR> framework with a view to achieving its adoption by reporting organisations round the world.

The framework employs the idea of plural 'capitals', which it defines as the resources and relationships an organisation uses or has an impact on. The 'capitals' include 'financial, manufactured, intellectual, human, social and relationship, and "natural" [as in the natural world] capital'.

The Sustainability Accounting Standards Board (SASB), based in San Francisco, is an independent, private-sector standards-setting organisation, 'dedicated to enhancing the efficiency of the capital markets', through the disclosure of sustainability information. It defines 'sustainability accounting' as reporting that reveals the environmental and social impacts of the firm's production of goods and services, and its 'management of the environmental and social capitals necessary to create long-term value'. Another independent standards-setter is the Global Reporting Initiative (GRI), which helps companies and governments to understand and report on their impact on corruption, human rights and climate change. By 2015, there were 7,500 organisations using GRI's Guidelines for sustainability reports.

With such a weight of attention, such a broadside of rankings and indices, and such a throng of experts thinking about and proposing reporting standards, it is no wonder large companies like Coca-Cola are taking ESG seriously. It is in their interests to act in ways that will improve their rankings in league tables and indices, and allow them to report favourably on their ESG performance, because a high ESG ranking reduces various kinds of risk, such as consumer boycotts and fines for breaches of regulations.

But they cannot spend too much on ESG compliance because, if they do, they will put their survival, and thus the sustainability of their ESG-compliant behaviour, at risk. They need to generate solid financial returns as well as the psychological returns that come from ESG compliance.

Without financial returns, there can be no returns at all for new paradigm investors.

Measuring impact

The closer an investment approach gets to simple philanthropy, the more pressing the need for measurement of non-financial returns, because without credible evidence of impact, an 'impact-first' fund (next to 'philanthropy' in the Bridges spectrum, see Chapter 6) will find it hard to attract new capital.

'Impact' investor Acumen (see p. 144) is developing what it calls a Lean Data system of customer-based benchmarks to measure the impacts of its investments in emerging markets. Energy is the first sector to which the system has been applied. The benchmarks include change in hours of daily study (enabled by lighting), cuts in household CO_2 emissions, reductions in kerosene lamp usage, improved safety and time savings. These impact measures say nothing about financial returns, of course. They are measures of the psychological returns that impact investors seek.

Programme evaluation and impact measurement are also of great interest to international organisations such as the World Bank, which know some of their aid programmes are ineffective but do not know which ones they are.

At present most 'impact' investing is in private markets, but it's likely that it will move to public markets if the measurement of impact improves, as it surely will.

According to Dr Dinah Koehler of UBS, some of the interesting new ideas for measuring impact are coming from wealthy philanthropists from the technology sector, 'because this is a group accustomed to measuring everything' (7.1). Koehler points to the contradiction in terms of measuring impact by input (see pp. 168–70). She says that: 'Just because money is invested in a social initiative doesn't mean that it will deliver a measurable positive impact.' And using inputs to measure impact does not take account of unintended side-effects: 'what if a water-treatment technology requires the use of a highly toxic chemical, which if released into the environment can cause health issues for humans?' she asks.

There is broad agreement that social impact should be measured in 'units of human well-being', as Koehler puts it. She says a promising approach here is to learn from the disciplines of public health and the environmental sciences, which have been involved in setting regulatory standards in these areas for decades. Companies that produce, store and sell goods all employ people, use energy and water and pollute air, water and soil. Their activities and the material, energy, water and pollutants that flow through them and from them, 'can be translated into units of human well-being using existing science', says Koehler.

Impact investors focus exclusively on the positive effects of the activities of their portfolio companies. That is okay for private markets, where companies are relatively small and have light footprints (carbon and otherwise). In public markets, where companies are larger and usually have heavier social and environmental footprints, there will be negative impacts that will have to be offset against the positive. If impact investing is to become established in public markets, those attracted by the basic idea will have to focus, not on positive impact, but on 'net-positive impact', after the negative impact has been subtracted.

Koehler and her colleagues are working with academics to find robust ways to measure impacts on climate change, water, food security and health. The research project is a partnership between UBS Asset Management and a large European pension fund.

Performance

An important matter for ESG investors is the penalty, if any, they should expect to incur in the form of lower financial returns if they restrict their investments to companies that comply with ESG criteria. In other words, what, if any, are the correlations between ESG compliance, and two variables: corporate financial performance and fund performance?

These are not easy questions to answer for at least three main reasons. First, because insufficient time has passed since the dawn of the ESG era to generate reliable data. Second, because messages conveyed by the data we do have remain equivocal. Third, because definitions of ESG vary, and there are no reliably objective means of establishing whether companies are abiding by espoused policies and principles.

Although the origins of ethical investing date back centuries, its modern era can be said to have begun barely a decade ago, with the unveiling of the six UN PRI in 2006 (see p. 17). And despite a great deal of research, it is still not clear whether or not the links between ESG, company financial and fund performance are causal. There is a correlation between ESG performance and fund and company financial performance (see below), but we do not yet know for sure that the former 'causes' the latter. Good ESG and financial performance could both be caused by something else, such as good management.

In an attempt to finesse the well-known 'correlation does not necessarily mean causation' problem, an MSCI study looked at how a company's ESG compliance might lead to good performance (7.2).

The study identified three 'transmission channels' within the discounted cash-flow (DCF) model: cash flow, 'idiosyncratic [firm-specific] risk' and 'valuation'. High ESG-rated companies transmit positive information to markets through the cash-flow channel when they are more competitive and earn abnormal returns. They transmit positive information through idiosyncratic risk channels because they are better at managing company-specific and operational risks. They transmit positive information through the valuation channel because they are less exposed to systematic risks. This leads to a lower cost of capital and thus to a higher DCF valuation.

But the lack of unequivocal proof of causality is of academic interest only. In the real world, the correlation is so strong, no serious error is likely to stem from assuming that there is a direct link between ESG compliance and good performance. And, ultimately, what does it matter if ESG compliance turns out to be a proxy for good management rather than a cause of good performance?

A more serious problem with the data is that ESG scores look more at the company's operational and organisational policies and structures than at its products or services. This explains why oil giant Shell, despite the greenhouse gas emissions caused by burning its main products, is usually more highly placed in ESG rankings than electric-car group Tesla, which does not have a formal ethics code or a governance policy. The other drawback of the ESG data is that they are limited, for the most part, to large, listed companies in mature markets and do not give the whole global picture.

It is also worth bearing in mind, when comparing the investment performance of ESG funds with the market, that ESG starts off with two handicaps. First, it is more expensive. The reporting and analysis of the ESG factors cost time and money. Specialised teams may be needed. Second, the ESG criteria will exclude from a portfolio some highly profitable companies that do not meet those criteria. In its race against the market, therefore, ESG investment is handicapped by an in-built performance deficit.

The evidence, however, suggests it is more than able to catch up. One study, commissioned by Deutsche Asset & Wealth Management Investment and published in 2015, found that: 'the business case for ESG investing is empirically well founded. Investing in ESG pays financially. Furthermore ... the positive ESG impact on CFP [corporate financial performance] is stable over time' (7.3).

This study has considerable authority because it is what the authors call a 'second-order meta-analysis'. In layman's terms, it combines and analyses the results of 60 'review' studies, each of which had combined and analysed the results of numerous empirical studies. Some of these review studies covered the same research as others, but this study indirectly incorporated the results of more than 2,200 unique empirical studies, dating back to the 1970s. The research found positive correlations between financial performance and all three of the ESG dimensions. The strongest link was with corporate governance: 10 per cent of the empirical studies found negative correlations between financial performance and governance, but 62 per cent found significant positive correlations.

The authors found some striking regional differences that led them to conclude there were 'ESG outperformance opportunities' in North America and emerging markets, in particular (see below).

Another review study undertaken by the University of Oxford's Smith School of Enterprise and the Environment and a sustainable investor, Arabesque Asset Management, reached similar conclusions. Some 90 per cent of the studies reviewed had found companies with high ESG standards enjoyed lower costs of capital; 88 per cent had found good ESG practices were associated with superior operating performance and 80 per cent had found stock price was correlated positively with those good practices (7.4). The authors concluded it was in the interests of investors and managers to incorporate ESG considerations in their decision-making, and predicted the future of sustainable investing lay in 'active ownership by multiple stakeholder groups, including investors and consumers' (our emphasis).

ESG and bond markets

The same positive correlations with ESG scores are evident in bond markets. A report by Barclays found that: 'the impact of ESG on the performance of US investment-grade corporate bonds in the past seven years [2009–16] has shown that portfolios that maximise ESG scores, while controlling for other risk factors have outperformed the index' (7.5). This outperformance was most pronounced for the governance component of ESG and least pronounced for the social component, but 'favouring issuers with strong Environmental or Social rating[s] has not been detrimental to bond returns'. The conclusions held using ESG ratings data from two ratings providers (MSCI ESG and Sustainalytics) with significantly different ratings methodologies.

The mind of the ESG investor

A study by Dutch academics seeking to shed light on 'the views and the actions of ESG managers' found that 'a large majority' of fund managers were signatories to the UN PRI, indicating that the influence of the PRI 'extends far beyond the domain of the group of managers who explicitly label or market themselves as socially responsible' (7.6).

Another insight was that ESG investors favour the analysis of companies over industries and that the 'strongest focus is on the governance of the firm, which has a close relationship with the quality of management'. The authors say that a 'successful realisation of an ESG policy requires a lot of strategic planning, because it directly relates to decisions with a long-term impact, including production technology ... use [of] natural resources, and the social dimension' and relationships with the employees and the community. 'Improper management of the environmental and social dimensions may have a serious, and negative impact on the ability of the firm to conduct its business'. G drives E and S, in other words.

The findings for professional investors were similar to those of earlier studies of retail investors, in that both consider ESG in a holistic way. The main difference is that professional asset managers see governance as more important than environmental and social factors, whereas retail investors regard 'environmental and sustainability issues' as the top priorities.

The research found that ESG investors had great confidence in their ability to generate positive risk-adjusted returns. In other words, they seem to see their investment approach as good business practice rather than the instrument of their desire to change the world. The authors did not say so, but it is, of course, possible to see ESG investing as both of these things simultaneously, and to believe that changing the world for the better *is* good business practice.

ESG is no guarantee

Not everything in the ESG garden is rosy. Investment in 'renewable energy', an example of ESG positive screening, has not been hugely rewarding in the past few years. Shares in Vestas, the Danish wind-turbine maker, more than doubled in price between 2014 and 2017, but in the same period, those of the world's largest wind-turbine maker, Xinjiang Goldwind, barely moved. China Longyuan Power, the largest user of wind power in China, was also a poor investment in the period (7.7).

A precipitous fall in the price of solar panels, many of them made in China, has made it hard for suppliers such as California-based SunPower, which makes most of its panels in the Philippines, Malaysia and Mexico, to make money. In the year to February 2018, its stock price fell 41 per cent, thanks partly to President Donald Trump's imposition of tariffs on imported solar panels.

For reasons such as these, specialised renewable energy funds such as BlackRock New Energy and Pictet's Clean Energy have underperformed in recent years. Part of the problem with the renewable energy sector has been too much money chasing too few high-quality investment opportunities.

It has also been suggested that the recent surge in so-called 'green' energy investment was partly fuelled by subsidies granted by national governments in their efforts to honour pledges made at the 2015 Paris Agreement on climate. When these subsidies are withdrawn, the green sceptics predict, the underlying economics of renewable energy, electric cars and other 'clean' technologies will turn out to be less attractive. An example of the subsidy 'solarcoaster', as Dan Whitten of the US Solar Energy Industries Association calls it, was the Chinese government's announcement in June 2018 that it was removing subsidies on most of its solar projects (7.8).

Sceptics also claim that in recent years 'green' energy funds have benefited from the impact on the financial performance of oil companies of lower oil prices and that when oil prices rise, as they surely will, oil companies will become relatively more profitable.

As a group, ESG-compliant companies and funds have performed well over the medium and long term, and are likely to continue to do so. But they are not and should not be expected to be immune to the vicissitudes of their political and economic environments, and of product and capital markets.

The academic literature provides comfort for those who worry about whether their ESG investing could be in breach of their fiduciary duties, but its exclusive focus on financial performance is like playing *Hamlet* without the prince. In this case, the absent prince is the psychological returns from ESG compliance: the value retail investors and fund beneficiaries derive from knowing their savings are being put to environmentally and socially responsible uses.

As we have seen, it is hard to measure the psychological returns from ESG investing but, if they were negligible, there would be no demand for ESG-sensitive investing. The fact that ESG investing is popular and becoming more so means that a growing number of people are willing to pay a financial price for the psychological returns it generates. And the fact that, as these studies show, they do not have to pay that price, means that ESG investing is a bargain. ESG investors in mature markets can have their cake and eat it, too.

The rewards of activism

Having presented evidence that ESG investment delivers better-than-market financial returns, we will turn to the question of whether 'active' investment management – the GSIA's seventh investment approach of 'corporate engagement' – can also deliver superior financial returns. We believe it can and does, but we are biased because it is what we do.

The University of Oxford and Arabesque literature review referred to above included various studies that found a 'momentum effect': strategies that assign a higher weight to companies with improving

ESG factors outperformed those focused on static ESG scores. The authors concluded from this result that logical investors could put pressure on their portfolio companies to boost their ESG scores, and so capture a momentum effect in the share price (7.4).

They cited another study by Elroy Dimson, Oğuzhan Karakaş and Xi Li (7.9), which found that companies that introduced changes after engagements with investors, outperformed. The study examined 613 US companies engaged by asset managers between 1999 and 2009. All were large and mature and underperforming before the start of the engagements. It took two to three engagements, each lasting 12–18 months, to achieve success, but it was worth the effort. The year after a successful corporate engagement, the investment return improved by an average of 7.1 per cent. The improvement was even better for engagements focused on corporate governance (an 8.6 per cent cumulative abnormal return), and better still (10.3 per cent cumulative abnormal return) for those focused on climate change.

After environmental and social engagements, returns on assets and sales per employee both improved significantly, suggesting an E or S engagement can improve customer and employee loyalty. 'Active ownership attenuates managerial myopia,' the authors deduced, and so helps to reduce losses caused by unforced management error and the company's vulnerability to unexpected external shocks.

The Dimson et al. study was pre-ESG and focused on ESG's most immediate antecedent, Corporate Social Responsibility. The authors concluded: 'Consistent with arguments that CSR activities attract socially conscious customers and investors, we find that, after successful engagements ... companies experience improvements in ... operating performance, profitability, efficiency and [corporate] governance.' The evidence suggests, therefore, that ESG investment outperforms the market and active investment also outperforms the market.

This conclusion is consistent with our own experience. We can point to many examples in our long careers as active investors in emerging markets of significant performance improvements following our engagements with our portfolio companies.

ESG in emerging markets

In the emerging markets, there is less local pressure on companies to improve their ESG performance. Most of the pressures come from ESG-sensitive foreign investors.

And because there is less readily available information about local companies, and less ESG reporting, it is harder for the ESG investor to calculate risks. ETFs are conspicuous by their absence from the share registers of emerging market companies because the coverage of EM indices is patchy. The MSCI EM benchmark index for emerging markets covers only two African countries – South Africa and Egypt.

However, the evidence, such as it is, suggests ESG investment in emerging markets performs well. MSCI's EM ESG Leaders Index has outperformed the MSCI EM benchmark consistently since the 2008/2009 financial crisis, and the outperformance has been increasing. In June 2017, it reached 51.84 points, double the difference in early 2013, and the gap continued to widen. By May 2018, it was within a whisker of 59 points above the benchmark. A dollar invested in the MSCI EM index in September 2007 was worth $1.23 in May

2018, but a dollar invested in the EM ESG Leaders Index was worth $1.82. This is a substantial outperformance.

The Leaders Index consists of 417 companies that score highly on ESG criteria as measured by MSCI. Chinese companies account for a quarter of its market capitalisation. The index excludes groups involved in alcohol, gambling, tobacco, nuclear power and weapons and 'tends to award lower ESG scores to companies with heavy state ownership and those in polluting industries, or with a poor record of labour relations' (7.10).

Alan Brett, an MSCI vice president, says correlations between governance and share price performance are clear: 'We see endemic underperformance among the SoEs [state-owned enterprises]. There is a very significant difference between them, and other ownership types, and this . . . is also evident in China.' He says that Chinese SoEs have 'a dual-track structure . . . who is pulling the strings? It is not the board . . . it all comes down to the [Communist] party.'

Our impression is that, although Brett has a point, things are improving for minority shareholders in Chinese SoEs (see p. 80). More generally, fund managers in emerging markets are conscious of the increasing importance local people are attaching to ESG issues in general and to E issues, in particular. 'What do Chinese people want?' asked Karine Hirn, partner at East Capital in Hong Kong, in an interview with the *Financial Times*. 'They dream of blue sky and blue water.'

The quantity and quality of data on, and analysis of, emerging markets and their companies are increasing all the time. It seems unlikely, however, despite steady improvements in the breadth and depth of information on companies in emerging markets, that ETFs or other passive funds will become powerful agents of change in these emerging economies. For all their size, passives do not pack enough punch because the signals they transmit by tracking one ESG index or another do not convey much useful information. Emerging market companies will not even be aware that they have been judged and found wanting by a passive ESG-screened fund, let alone why. Only active funds pursuing corporate engagement policies can exert ESG-related influence on emerging market companies.

The performance evidence presented here allows us to answer all of the three questions with which we began this book. There is 'money' in ESG investing; there is 'money' in active investing; and there is 'money' in ESG investing in emerging markets. There is insufficient evidence to demonstrate clearly that there is 'money' in active ESG investing in emerging markets, but given the other evidence, it is likely that there is even more money in this investment approach.

Doing good

The negative-screening approach to ESG of passive funds (companies that do not pass the ESG test, do not get into the portfolio) is a weakness for millennials, because their objective is to change the world, not to judge it. They want action on environmental, social and governance issues, and emerging markets is where action can do the most good. There are measurement problems to be sure, but here as elsewhere, it is better to be roughly right than precisely wrong. When it comes to ESG, it is sometimes enough to know you are on the side of the angels.

For those who care about the ESG issues, companies that would fail ESG tests at the time of the investment, but with prodding by active investors could pass them subsequently, may well offer the highest composite (financial + psychological) returns. Sub-Saharan Africa teems with such companies (see Chapter 8).

Although they do not seem to need to, millennials are willing to pay extra for ESG compliance, in lower pay as employees, higher prices as consumers and lower returns as savers. But they are not writing blank cheques. They want performance as well as compliance with the ESG agenda.

Companies in all regions of the world, including the emerging markets, are trying to deliver high-composite (earnings + impact) returns. There is no cause for cynicism about how they are reacting to the ESG pressures exerted by the millennial generation, and no reason to question their motives or doubt their sincerity as they respond to the growing chorus of ESG evangelism and the increased scrutiny of corporate ESG performance. What really matters is that actions are being taken and commitments are being made. Moreover, if the true measure of a company's beliefs about the environment, social justice in the supply chain and the quality of corporate governance is a mosaic of the beliefs of the people who work for or with it, a growing proportion of whom are 'millennials', it is hard not to see these companies themselves as bona fide members of the *Blue Planet 2* generation.

8

The great awakening

If the growing number of people alive today who are not struggling to survive were asked to name the most pressing issues of our age, the environment would be close to the top of the list. A planetary consciousness has emerged in the past few decades. The belief that what people do affects natural systems is now firmly embedded in the global psyche. Most people believe the climate is changing for the worse and it is partly our fault. Most people have been alarmed by revelations about the impact of plastic waste on wildlife and the oceans. We are ashamed of the 'dead zones' we have created in our seas and lakes. Satellite images show the alarming contraction of our rainforests, coral reefs, glaciers and ice shelves and the expansion of deserts. The Sahara and Gobi deserts are both growing by thousands of square kilometres each year. Air pollution obliges millions of people to breathe through face masks.

Another issue close to the top of the 'most pressing' list is what Scottish poet Robert Burns called 'man's inhumanity to man'. People are outraged by stories of human trafficking, child labour, derisory wages and appalling working conditions in plantations in Africa and South America, and the sweatshops of South East Asia and the Indian subcontinent. Shocking fatalities and casualties as a result of fires and the collapse of factory buildings attest to a disgraceful disregard for the health and safety of workers. Anger at such inhumanity turns to shame when people in mature economies realise that it supports their own lifestyles.

A third issue that arouses our indignation and disgust is the greed, dishonesty and irresponsibility of powerful people. We are appalled by the apparent impunity with which predatory elites and corrupt officials steal from the weak, plunder national treasuries and condemn their fellow citizens to lives of poverty and fear. We see in these gangsters and warlords, masquerading as governments, the origin of the waves of refugees and illegal immigrants, testing the patience of electorates of more stable and prosperous states.

Public anger at failings of governance is not only directed at emerging market nations. People everywhere want the governance of their institutions to be fair, honest, law-abiding and efficient. They are just as incensed, if not more so, by the revelations that German carmaker Volkswagen used so-called 'defeat devices' on its diesel engines to evade environmental protection regulation, as by the scandals that have affected companies such as Petrobras, Asia Pulp and Paper, and Samsung.

Ours is a far from perfect world for people in their roles as consumers, employees and investors. But there is, at least, at the end of the second decade of the twenty-first century, an emerging consensus about the priorities for reform. There is broad agreement now that our institutions must endeavour to become more environmentally and socially responsible, and should try to ensure their governance is fair, law-abiding and efficient.

Some will argue this new emphasis on responsibility and moral obligations is too puritanical, and that, in the real world, we must learn to live with a little sin. We do not agree. There can be no compromises in the pursuit of the ESG agenda, no wriggle room for those inclined to ignore their responsibilities or pay no heed to moral imperatives. We are uncompromising ESG investors because we know irresponsibility and a willingness to countenance immoral behaviour translates directly into costs for companies and losses for investors. By the time of writing, in summer 2018, Volkswagen had paid $26 billion in penalties since the defeat devices scandal broke in March 2015. More to the point for investors, concern about the impact of the scandal on the business caused the VW share price that year to plummet from over €246 in March to less than €96 in November. The shares have rallied since, but in mid-2018 the price was still more than €100 below its 2015 peak.

All roads lead to ESG

Those who expect ESG investing to turn out to be another fad – like tulips, the South Sea Company or the dot com craze at the end of the twentieth century, that burns brightly for a little while but fades away when the market's attention shifts to other fads such as the 'Internet of Things' or artificial intelligence – are mistaken.

ESG investing is still largely a European phenomenon, fuelled by European money, but its share of the worldwide asset management market is growing fast. We expect that, by 2050, all investment will be ESG-screened in one way or another, and that companies that do not comply and show no prospect of complying with what will by then be far more sophisticated ESG tests, will not have access to global capital.

There are two reasons for our confidence in the durability of the ESG approach to investing: it is a strong brand that is in tune with the zeitgeist, and it is a profitable investment strategy.

A great strength of ESG as a brand is that it is very hard to attack. No one, or at least no government, could publicly object to its assertions: organisations should behave in environmentally and socially responsible ways, and both companies and countries should be well and fairly governed.

Another strength is the way the three components support each other. 'E' is the marketing spearhead: pictures of shrinking ice shelfs and glaciers; face masks in cities under a penumbra of thick poisonous fog; contaminated ground and rain water; mountains of plastic rubbish in and around cities; plastic-littered beaches; plastic-clogged rivers and estuaries; windblown plastic sheets, caught in trees and draped over hedgerows. In addition to provoking feelings of alarm, dismay, anger and revulsion, such images beg 'why?', 'how?' and 'who?' questions. In seeking answers, people find 'S' images of child labour, sweatshop blazes and collapsed factory buildings. The heat of opposition to the status quo begins to rise. ESG becomes a rallying cry.

Like all strong brands, ESG builds a bridge between minds and markets, across which flow beliefs, desires and intentions. But the strength of the ESG brand would count for next to nothing in the investment marketplace, if there was clear evidence that ESG investment strategies perform poorly. There is no such evidence. On the contrary, as we saw in the previous chapter, the vast majority of thousands of studies found strong positive correlations between ESG and ESG-like investment approaches and fund performance.

This is both surprising at first sight and significant. It is surprising because, other things being equal, one would expect an investment strategy that imposes non-financial restrictions on stock selection to underperform the market. The findings are also significant because they remove the most formidable objection to the adoption of ESG investment strategies, namely the fiduciary duty of fund managers always to act in the interests of the fund's beneficiaries. If ESG investment strategies outperform the market, fund managers are not only entitled to adopt them, but are also obliged by their fiduciary duty to do so.

On reflection, it is not so surprising that companies and fund management firms that adopt ESG policies outperform. A management team guided by moral precepts and a sense of responsibility would not have dreamed of allowing the use of a device designed to cheat in emissions tests. Similarly, an ESG fund manager who had heard that a company was up to some such trick would not have dreamed of investing in it.

ESG is a nexus. The term has emerged from the fund management community, but it has a wider significance. It brings together not only hitherto unconnected themes, but also previously unconnected communities. It maps out common ground for consumers worried about the environment and the social impact of global supply chains, for enlightened managers concerned about their companies' reputations and for active investors seeking to maximise risk-adjusted returns on their investments, particularly in emerging markets.

As we saw in Chapter 6, various types of players are active in emerging markets. Not-for-profits focus on urgent needs and expect nothing economic in return; so-called 'impact' funds focus on the UN's 17 Sustainable Development Goals (SDGs), invest in private markets and expect some economic return; 'active' ESG funds invest in public markets, engage with managements and seek a market-rate or better return; some 'passive' funds track ESG indices that have limited coverage of emerging markets; and traditional funds, which impose no constraint on where or in what they invest, occasionally dabble in emerging markets when opportunities are obvious.

Active and 'activist' funds occasionally get together to put pressure on management teams and fight 'proxy battles', but there has so far been very little collaboration between various types of investor and between investors and other interested parties, such as customers and consumers.

It has been suggested 'active' investors could increase their power by acting in concert with consumers on common ground, mapped out by ESG. 'In our view,' Gordon Clark, Andreas Feiner and Michael Viehs have suggested, 'the next step in the evolution of active ownership is to include the ultimate beneficiaries of [active funds] who are at the same time, the ultimate consumers of the goods and services of the invested companies, into the agenda and priority-setting process' (8.1). There may also be other possibilities for similar cooperation in emerging markets, along the Bridges spectrum (see Chapter 6), such as between 'impact' and 'active' investors.

Such collaboration and concerted action under the umbrella of the ESG brand could become a powerful addition to the arsenals of active investors. Proxy battles in shareholder meetings, backed up by synchronised and vociferous consumer protests on the street and in social media, all demanding ESG-related reforms, would be a serious challenge for obdurate management teams or self-interested majority shareholders.

ESG is the mantra, the common ground on which these disparate groups, each of which is an aspect of the spirit of the times, can make common cause. The message for the investor is clear: 'Don't bet against the zeitgeist.'

No hiding place

The ESG zeitgeist has emerged from the concerns of ordinary people about certain environmental, social and governance aspects of the modern world. It is conventional to attribute these concerns to the 'millennial' generation, but ESG sensitivities are not confined to people born between 1980 and 1995.

Studies suggest that millennials are more concerned about ESG issues than other generations, but not dramatically so. Their real importance lies elsewhere and is twofold. First, because they are a very large generation, entering the high-earning periods of their lives, the choices they make about what to buy and where to work have great economic significance for companies all over the world. Second, because they are the most communicative generation the world has ever seen, their decisions are more coherent and better informed than those of previous generations. In the past, corrupt or otherwise delinquent managers and officials could hide behind a veil of ignorance protecting their misdeeds from public scrutiny. Nowadays, that is not so easy. The smartphone and social media, of which millennials are the most active users, can illuminate the darkest corners of business and government.

News, news analysis, fake news, rumour and suspicions spread like wildfire, through a proliferation of news channels, blogs and mass-market social media platforms. This more or less constant communication maintains the momentum of movements and protests and obliges organisations, more used to the monologue of press releases and statements, to engage in dialogue and debate.

It is true that oratory and eloquence have become the victims in a world in which the sheer quantity of communication overwhelms the quality. The Twitter activity of US President Donald Trump is a case in point. He maintains the loyalty of his supporters by tweeting a constant stream of aggressive, poorly written, and often unsubstantiated assertions or accusations, usually ending in a brief capitalised message.

But there are 'signals' as well as 'noise' in this cacophony of social media chit-chat. There is an insistence on openness these days. Secrecy is outmoded. From being a 'snitch' or a 'grass', the whistle-blower has become a champion of transparency and a hero of the Information Age. It is a more hostile environment for those who break the letter or the spirit of the law, engage in corrupt and irresponsible practices and take no notice of popular demands for ESG compliance.

In addition to being the dominant consumers of our time, these communicative, curious and well-informed people are fast becoming the dominant investors. How likely is it that people who take care to buy sneakers made of plastic garbage salvaged from the oceans will be content to be passive investors? We expect them to favour active managers who will do battle for them with boards to demand compliance with the ESG creed.

ESG investing for everyone

Time was when ESG investing was a niche activity. Not anymore. The GSIA estimated that over a quarter of assets worldwide ($23 trillion, in total) were being 'sustainably' managed, in one way or another, in 2016 (see Chapter 1). Since then, the figure has grown, and several new ESG-screened indices have been launched. The information is out there for those who want to apply ESG principles to their investments – so are the funds and, for 'passive' investors, so are the indices for tracker funds to follow.

As we have said, however, we do not believe people with mastery of ever smarter smartphones, familiarity with the social media and an insatiable, ESG-guided curiosity will be content with a passive approach to investment. Over the next few years, we expect smartphones and social media to generate huge amounts of raw data on ESG performance. The data will be analysed by investors and their research consultants and turned into information. So-called Key Performance Indicators (KPIs) will be developed for scores of ESG subcategories and from these KPIs comprehensive ESG scorecards will emerge, revealing the company's ESG strengths and weaknesses in great detail.

It will not be long before all companies and funds in the mature markets are ranked on a range of ESG-related KPIs on a new kind of share-comparison website that will allow investors to set up their own tests for inclusion in their portfolios. If you are more concerned about a company's carbon footprint than the median wage it pays its employees, for instance, give the former more weight in your comparison searches.

Collectively, this new generation of investors are defining in ever greater detail what they expect in return from companies they invest in. Corrupt and incompetent senior managers are running out of places to hide.

In practice, emerging markets investors have choices. Although few can afford to be active investors themselves and travel round the world engaging with the companies they invest in, they can spend time seeking out ESG bargains on tipster blogs, IMF and World Bank statistics, Transparency International and Ibrahim Foundation league tables, investor news channels, price-comparison websites, etc., and applying their negative and positive screening tests and weightings. Or they can delegate the stock-picking tasks to investment professionals, human or otherwise. There are plenty to choose from.

At present, ESG compliance for most passive funds consists of little more than box-ticking. If the index a passive fund chooses to track has 'ESG' in its name, that is job done. No attempts are made to measure, with any precision, the ESG impact of a portfolio company or how it compares with other companies in its peer group. That there is a hunger for better measures of ESG factors and of contributions to meeting the UN's SDGs is demonstrated by the success of specialist research firms such as Sustainalytics. It is generally recognised, however, that not enough has been invested in the expensive process of gathering raw data on ESG performance, particularly in emerging markets.

The lack so far of precise ESG metrics is felt most keenly at the 'impact' end of the spectrum of capital, because that is where non-financial ESG returns are most important to investors. For those attracted by the higher ESG impacts in emerging markets, where ESG information is harder to come by, the choice of funds is limited to the 'active' ESG funds that compensate for the relative lack of information by engaging directly with boards and management teams.

Governance is the key

We have argued in this book that governance is the prime driver of ESG because, without good governance and the good management that it fosters, environmentally and socially responsible policies are unlikely to be adopted and implemented. By 'good' governance, we mean a particular set of corporate governance principles that some may characterise as 'Western', but which we regard as universal, in that they emerge from the logic of the business situation.

The principles should be familiar by now, but let us summarise them once more. Good corporate governance is:

- Fair, in that all shareholders are treated equally.

- Open, in that all relevant information is disclosed to all shareholders at the same time.

- Aligned, in that the interests of the company's management are the same as those of shareholders.

- Based on rules that are generally complied with.

The hunger of emerging market companies for capital puts them under pressure to respect these governance principles because, if they do not, they will be denied access to the mobile pool of global capital. Companies that adopt and abide by these basic principles do more than make themselves attractive to foreign investors. They also import – by the back door, so to speak – a concept of governance that is as applicable to governments as it is to companies.

They establish within a society a sometimes subversive set of ideas: government must be 'fair', in that citizens must be treated equally; it must be 'open', in that major policy decisions must be approved, or rejected by a parliament; it must be 'aligned' with the interests of the people, in that governments must be chosen by them in free and fair elections; it must be 'rules-based', in that property rights are respected, and all citizens are equal before a body of law administered by an independent judiciary.

In short, we believe local business leaders who recognise the merits of, and sign up to, the ESG principles, will put pressure on governments to reform themselves and invigorate their economies. Wherever they take root, ESG principles create a general hunger for more stable, responsible, even-handed and efficient government. An example of this 'overspill' of ESG principles from companies into the political sphere was the transformation of Lagos after the seat of government was moved inland and the city's administration was left in the hands of business people (see p. 94).

We are not saying the infusion of ESG principles into politics and government creates the ideal form of government. We are saying it creates a form of government that is attractive to companies and foreign investors.

Images of good governance are hard to come by, but one sticks in our minds: a picture of the Public Service Hall in Tbilisi, the capital of Georgia, with its roof of huge white mushrooms standing on slender white stems, covering a glass office block, symbolising open and transparent government (see Chapter 4).

The promise of emerging markets

Just as fishermen favour previously unfished waters, so ESG-guided investors eager to maximise their impact tend to favour companies and places where ESG standards are relatively low because that is where their ESG evangelism can make the most difference.

Emerging markets are prime territory for active investors who are keen to earn ESG as well as financial returns. Emerging market countries dominate the lower ranks of Transparency International's CPI (see p. 64) and the hunger of emerging market companies for foreign capital makes them unusually amenable to demands for ESG compliance.

Companies in emerging markets also have other attractions for ESG investors. We mentioned in Chapter 1 the opportunities for leap-frogging stages of economic development. The availability of technologies developed in mature markets, for instance, enables emerging market countries to skip the wired stages of telecommunications and go straight to wireless and the vast communicative spaces created by broadband Internet. New energy technologies may also enable countries in emerging markets to leap-frog traditional stages of energy development, and go straight to 'smart', local mini-grids using renewable energy.

In just the same way, with the help of a vast library of case study material accumulated by Western business schools, developing countries have been able to start lower down the learning curve of management. We must emphasise again that this is not to say the US style of management, or the European style, with its stronger ESG emphasis, is 'better' than other styles in a fundamental sense. It is simply the standard by which the gatekeepers of the mobile pool of global capital judge the quality of management and governance.

One important group of missionaries from mature economies are the subsidiaries and associates of global companies. Some of them are required by local laws to be majority-owned by natives, but they are all managed by their foreign partners according to general principles widely adhered to in mature markets.

They are like Trojan horses, containing teams of executives who believe in and promote the Western way of doing things in all the territories where they operate. And, increasingly these days, this Western way of doing things is ESG-compliant.

These blessings are not unmixed, however. When pursuing their global ambitions, multinationals sometimes use their actual or de facto control over local subsidiaries for the benefit of their own shareholders at the expense of their local co-investors. They may pay lower dividends than the parent, use transfer pricing to move profits to lower-tax jurisdictions or impose high central services fees and exorbitant royalties for the use of brand names.

On balance, however, we think most multinational subsidiaries and associates in the emerging markets make positive contributions to their host countries' economic development.

Consider Africa

It is not fashionable to be optimistic about Africa. To many in the West, the continent still seems plagued by war, famine and waves of pestilence; its primitive economies can seem riddled with corruption; its wealth is subject to wholesale theft by avaricious elites, who salt their plunder away in tax havens.

We see Africa differently. Africa is a big economic story, maybe the biggest in our lifetime. Future historians may compare it with the industrialisation of China after Deng Xiaoping's 'great opening' in 1978. Africa's population is expected to double to 2.4 billion by 2050. If the continent's GDP per head is approaching the current European level by then, the African economy will be about three times the current size of Europe's.

We have been lucky enough to have travelled all over Africa, investing on the west and east coasts and even in Zimbabwe. For investors, there are pearls to be found everywhere in Africa. It is a very exciting, high-risk, high-reward area, where corruption at the highest levels remains rampant, but, at the same time, the ambitions and attitudes of ordinary people are becoming wider and more positive. An 18-year-old Kenyan boy can be more hopeful about his future than his parents were at his age because there is more stability and transparency. He or his sister may even be attracted by the idea of starting his or her own engineering business.

It is important not to judge – not to bemoan the lack of well-regulated markets or to marvel at the fragility of property rights in a particular country. The challenge is to describe and identify the structural changes that are taking place: the impact of modern telecommunications, the inclusion of people in the economy through mobile phones who were previously excluded, the much wider range of business models created by the Internet and the smartphone, and the improved access of small businesses to energy and money.

From all this activity and optimism in the undergrowth of the fastest-growing economies in sub-Saharan Africa, systems of checks and balances are emerging spontaneously, reflecting the increasing numbers of people who have a vested interest in stability.

When we enter a country, seeking investment opportunities, we engage with local people at the sub-political level: with bankers, C-level executives, financial institutions, entrepreneurs. In many African countries, but sadly not all, we see these financial and business people creating the corporations and putting together the institutional frameworks of well-ordered market economies. There are 29 stock exchanges in Africa now, plus a handful of commodity exchanges. Most of the sub-Saharan exchanges have been set up over the past two decades.

The main governance risks in Africa these days are associated more with central banks and politics than with local companies. In our experience, the private sectors in Africa are far ahead of public sectors in developing rule-based systems. You can invest with more confidence in a brewery in Kenya or a bank in Togo than sovereign lenders can when making loans to some African governments.

There are often two kinds of upside here: the rapid growth of some African economies, and a parallel improvement in the quality of their governance. 'A rising tide lifts all ships,' as the saying goes. Improving corporate governance standards in a country should lift all sound companies and reduce the country's risk premium.

Many investors steer clear of Africa because there is so much uncertainty. They are attracted by the high growth rates, but are fearful of the crises that can suddenly erupt out of the blue when there is a military coup or some other political realignment. We are more sanguine about crises because our experience has taught us that they are more likely to herald periods of reform and improvement than periods of regression or deterioration.

The active advantage

An irony of today's investment world is that ESG investing – a new kind of active discrimination in investment – is spreading at the same time as a general retreat from active investing, demonstrated by the growth of passive funds.

This disconnect is particularly acute in the emerging markets where investment opportunities are greatest, but the institutional infrastructures (property rights, independent judiciary, etc.) are weakest. Passive funds cannot cope with institutional weaknesses. All they can do is track emerging market indices that, because of a general lack of information, do not cover less advanced emerging market countries. Only active investors, ready and willing to use their influence directly and continuously to press their portfolio companies to improve their governance, can bridge this gap between opportunity and risk in emerging markets.

We say 'continuously' because it is not enough to do your due diligence before investing. Active investors must continue to keep a watchful eye on portfolio companies after investment, from the vantage point of a non-executive seat on the board, if appropriate and possible, or as a vigilant and, if necessary, a vocal minority shareholder.

Continued post-investment vigilance is necessary because it is one thing for a company to make ESG commitments to a new investor, and quite another for a company to deliver on such ESG commitments in the medium to long term. But the evidence suggests it is worth it. Dimson, Karakaş and Li found prolonged corporate engagements deliver abnormal returns (see Chapter 7). In their study of 613 US companies, they found that, on average, engagements focused on corporate governance delivered an 8.6 per cent cumulative abnormal return.

This is entirely consistent with our own combined 80 years of experience investing in emerging markets and working on governance issues in portfolio companies. We have seen at first hand the successful change such engagement can inspire and the returns it can generate. Three decades ago, Mark launched the first London-listed emerging markets investment trust. A focus on corporate governance was a core theme from the outset. The portfolio he put together remains to this day one of the most successful emerging market funds. The total NAV return since the fund's launch in 1989 until Mark's departure in 2015 was over 1950 per cent against a return of about 700% of the MSCI Emerging Markets Index (8.2).

The growth of passive investing suggests that, in the rivalry between humans and algorithms, the latter have the edge in mature markets, thanks partly to widespread 'greenwashing' (box-ticking) in alleged ESG investing. But algorithms are data-hungry and there are not enough data to automate investment in emerging markets.

It is possible that, eventually, there will be enough data on the emerging markets to satisfy the hunger of investment algorithms. That is decades away, however, and it is hard to imagine algorithms engaging with companies on their governance and ESG compliance in general, in the same way as active human investors. Human interactions and engagement and the mutual trust they engender are the essence of successful emerging markets investment.

We remain confident that as active investors we play a vital role in the market. Now is the time to be championing ESG standards across emerging markets as they begin to flourish on the global stage. Companies want it, consumers expect it and we as investors should demand it. This is how we can make a difference over the long term. This is how we invest for good.

REFERENCES

I.1 Ian Prior, 'Boomers vs. Millennials', US Trust, *Capital Acumen*, 33, 2018.

1.1 GSIA, *2016: Global Sustainable Investment Review*, 2017.

1.2 David Pilling, 'How free trade could unlock Africa's potential', *Financial Times*, 4 April 2018.

2.1 NOAA, 'Gulf of Mexico "dead zone" predictions feature uncertainty', 21 June 2012.

2.2 Martin Wolf, 'How to make a carbon pricing system work', *Financial Times*, 29 March 2018.

2.3 'Ali Enterprises: A factory inferno', https://cleanclothes.org/safety/ali-enterprises.

2.4 Department for International Development and Foreign and Commonwealth Office, 'A case study on the Rana Plaza disaster in Bangladesh from the 2013 Human Rights and Democracy Report', London, 10 April 2014.

2.5 ILO, 'Forced labour, human trafficking and slavery', www.ilo.org/global/topics/forced-labour/lang--en/index.htm, 6 February 2015.

2.6 Richard Milne, 'Norway's oil fund sells out of Warren Buffett-owned utility', *Financial Times*, 10 July 2018.

2.7 Leon Kaye, 'Venture fund launched to fight human rights violations in global supply chains', *TriplePundit*, 15 February 2018.

2.8 'Suicides at Foxconn: Light and death', *The Economist*, 27 May 2010.

2.9 John Paczkowski, 'Apple CEO Steve Jobs live at D8: All we want to do is make better products', http://allthingsd.com/20100601/steve-jobs-session/, 1 June 2010.

3.1 Sarah Murray, 'Mo Ibrahim: "It is the head of the fish that goes rotten first"', *Financial Times*, 15 November 2017.

3.2 Mario Macis, 'Gender differences in wage and leadership', *IZA World of Labor*, 2017.

3.3 World Economic Forum, *The Global Gender Gap Report* 2018, Geneva, 2018.

3.4 Macis, 'Gender differences', 2017.

3.5 MGI, *The Power of Parity: How Advancing Women's Equality Can Add $12 Trillion to Global Growth*, September 2015.

3.6 *PwC Women in Work Index: Closing the Gender Pay Gap*, PwC UK, March 2016.

3.7 Marcus Noland, Tyler Moran and Barbara Kotschwar, 'Is gender diversity profitable? Evidence from a global survey', *Working Paper Series*, WP 16–3, Peterson Institute of International Economics, February 2016.

3.8 Vivian Hunt, Sara Prince, Sundiatu Dixon-Fyle and Lareina Yee, *Delivering through Diversity*, McKinsey & Company, January 2018.

3.9 World Economic Forum, *The Global Gender Gap Report 2018*.

3.10 The Philanthropic Initiative, *Women Leading the Way in Impact Investing*, 2018; and US Trust, *2016 US Trust Insights on Wealth and Worth: Annual Survey of High-Net-Worth and Ultra-High-Net-Worth Americans*, Bank of America Corporation, 2016.

3.11 Anjli Raval, 'Aramco IPO puts Saudi Arabia's grand vision to the test', *Financial Times*, 2 May 2018.

3.12 Reuters, 13 August 2015.

3.13 Carsten Huber, *unFAIR PLAY! Labour Relations at Hyundai: A Critical Review*, Geneva: IndustriAll Global Union, April 2014.

3.14 Bryan Harris, 'Foreign funds force Hyundai to "re-evaluate" $8.8bn restructuring', *Financial Times*, 22 May 2018.

3.15 Karl R. Popper, *The Open Society and Its Enemies*, Vol. 1, 5th edn, Princeton, NJ: Princeton University Press, 1966.

3.16 Gianni Montezemolo, *Europe Incorporated: The New Challenge*, Chichester: John Wiley and Sons, 2000.

4.1 David Pilling, 'Why Lagos works', *Financial Times*, 25 March 2018.

5.1 Adam Smith, *An Inquiry into the Nature and Causes of the Wealth of Nations*, London: Ward, Lock, 1875; originally published 1776.

5.2 Adolf A. Berle, *Power without Property: A New Development in American Political Economy*, New York: Harcourt Brace, 1959.

5.3 Nicola Bullock, 'Investors hail S&P 500 move over multiple class shares', *Financial Times*, 1 August 2017.

5.4 Caroline Binham and Anjli Raval, 'UK presses ahead on listing reforms in effort to woo Saudi Aramco', *Financial Times*, 8 June 2018.

5.5 Claudio R. Rojas, 'Eclipse of the public corporation revisited: Concentrated equity ownership theory', *Oxford Business Law Blog*, Faculty of Law, University of Oxford, 22 June 2017.

5.6 Sahil Mahtani, 'Groupe Bolloré and Elliott go head-to-head over Telecom Italia', *Financial Times*, 3 May 2018.

5.7 John Aglionby, Anna Nicolaou and Scheherazade Daneshkhu, 'Consumer goods groups join war on plastic', *Financial Times*, 22 January 2018.

5.8 Leslie Hook, 'Big business in UK pledges to cut plastic packaging', *Financial Times*, 26 April 2018.

6.1 Susanna Rust, 'A new frontier?', *Investment & Pensions Europe*, May 2017.

6.2 Gillian Tett, 'Impact investing for good and market returns', *Financial Times*, 14 December 2017.

6.3 www.impactsummiteurope.com.

6.4 GSIA, *2016: Global Sustainable Investment Review*, 2017.

6.5 Acumen, *Energy Impact Report*, 2017.

6.6 Rob Matheson, 'Study: Mobile-money services lift Kenyans out of poverty', MIT News Office, 8 December 2016.

6.7 Egon Vavrek, 'ESG in emerging markets depends on better data and disclosure', *Financial Times*, 24 July 2017.

6.8 David Stevenson, 'Ethical investing is not just for millennials', *Financial Times*, 9 January 2018.

6.9 *Industrialize Africa: Strategies, Policies, Institutions, and Financing*, Abidjan: African Development Bank Group, 2017.

7.1 Dr D. A. Koehler, 'Changing finance, financing change: The advent of impact measurement for public equities', *Investment & Pensions Europe*, May 2017.

7.2 Guido Giese, Linda-Eling Lee, Dimitris Melas, Zoltan Nagy and Laura Nishikawa, 'Foundations of ESG Investing, Part 1: How ESG affects equity valuation, risk and performance', *Research Insight: MSCI ESG Research LLC*, MSCI, November 2017.

7.3 Gunnar Friede, Timo Busch and Alexander Bassen, 'ESG and financial performance: Aggregated evidence from more than 2000 empirical studies', *Journal of Sustainable Finance & Investment*, 2015, 210–33.

7.4 Gordon Clark, Andreas Feiner and Michael Viehs, 'From the stockholder to the stakeholder: How sustainability can drive financial outperformance', University of Oxford and Arabesque Partners, March 2015.

7.5 Barclays, 'Sustainable investing and bond returns: Research study into the impact of ESG on credit portfolio performance', *Impact Series*, 01, London: Barclays Bank, 2016.

7.6 Emiel van Duuren, Auke Plantinga and Bert Scholtens, 'ESG integration and the investment management process: Fundamental investing reinvented', *Journal of Business Ethics*, 138 (3), 2016, 525–33.

7.7 Alan Livsey, 'Green is not always good for investors', *Financial Times*, 13 September 2017.

7.8 Leslie Hook and Lucy Hornby, 'China's solar desire dims', *Financial Times*, 8 June 2018.

7.9 Elroy Dimson, Oğuzhan Karakaş and Xi Li, 'Active ownership', *Review of Financial Studies*, 28 (12), 2015 (posted October 2012).

7.10 James Kynge, 'Investors in companies that do good do better', *Financial Times*, 20 July 2017.

8.1 Gordon Clark, Andreas Feiner and Michael Viehs, 'From the stockholder to the stakeholder: How sustainability can drive financial outperformance', University of Oxford and Arabesque Partners, March 2015.

8.2 Source: Bloomberg.

INDEX

Content in tables is indicated with the suffix t, and in boxes with the suffix b.